Pebble Beach Concours d'Elegance

The Art of the Poster

Ford Motor Company,
on the occasion of its Centennial,
is pleased to have helped make this
book possible.

Pebble Beach Concours d'Elegance

The Art of the Poster

Robert T. Devlin
with Kandace Hawkinson

Dalton Watson Fine Books
Deerfield, Illinois, USA • Ferring, Sussex, England

Published by Dalton Watson Fine Books, Ltd.
www.daltonwatson.com
email: info@daltonwatson.com

1 Arundel Court, Elverlands Close
Ferring, W. Sussex BN12 5QE
England

1730 Christopher Drive
Deerfield, IL 60015
USA

Printed and bound in England by The Lavenham Press
Book design by Queener Design, USA

Devlin, Robert T.
Pebble Beach Concours d'Elegance. The Art of the Poster.

ISBN 1-85443-201-X (case bound)
ISBN 1-85443-202-8 (leather bound)

Contents

GWENN GRAHAM
DEL MONTE LODGE PEBBLE BEACH
CONCOURS
BENEFIT COMMUNITY HOSPITAL AUXILIARY 1969
MAY 31

Foreword

■ THE CONCOURS D'ELEGANCE—LITERALLY, "PARADE OF ELEGANCE"—began at a time when motorcars were only for the privileged few, and cars were judged in large part on the basis of how well they paired with the fashions and pedigrees of their owners.

One man and one car changed all that. Henry Ford's Model T brought the freedom of personal transportation to the world at large. And now the automobile is celebrated not as a mere accessory, but as an important creation that has changed the way we live our lives. It has allowed us to dream new dreams—and pursue them.

Pebble Beach is concours d'elegance at its best. "Pebble" is where enthusiasts from around the world gather to see the most beautiful, innovative and rare examples of the automobile. The variety is staggering. Classic luxury cars, among them custom-built Fords and Lincolns, pose beside historic hot rods. It is a grand celebration of the car as both mechanical wonder and art—as kinetic sculpture translating energy and motion into beauty.

Each year since its founding more than one half century back, the Pebble Beach Concours d'Elegance has distilled this celebration in a commemorative poster. These posters are now highly prized not just as mementos, but as artwork in their own right. The poster artists have offered us unique visions and insights, while consistently capturing the importance, the elegance, and the joy of the automobile.

In celebration of Ford Motor Company's 100th anniversary, and on behalf of the Ford family, we are pleased to sponsor this retrospective look at the Pebble Beach Concours d'Elegance posters.

Edsel B. Ford II

To my parents, Arthur Coghlan Devlin and Dorothy Eleanor Valentine Devlin,
in fond memory of what they brought to all interactions with others – humor, respect, intelligence and, above all else, style.

Robert T. Devlin

Author's Note

■ THIS BOOK DERIVES FROM THREE DEEP PASSIONS: MY FERVOR FOR AUTOMOBILES, MY APPRECIATION OF FINE ART, and my longtime interest in history. I feel fortunate to be able to put these words to paper, to have been given this opportunity to share my passions with others.

The Influence of Automobiles and Art on My Life

Cars have brought much joy to my life. I restored my first car—a 1931 Ford Model A Victoria Coupé—at the age of eleven. Technically, I was not yet old enough to drive, but I must admit that I did manage a few laps around the block. Many restorations followed, and I'm proud to say that a few of these efforts were ultimately displayed at that most elegant of all automotive events, the Pebble Beach Concours d'Elegance.

I first attended the Pebble Beach Concours back in 1952, soon after my parents acquired a summer home on the Monterey Peninsula. The Concours was still in its infancy then; it was paired with the Pebble Beach Road Race, and it was the latter event that was the big draw. But I did attend both events, and I still remember them. I recall the rush I felt watching racecars barrel around the tight twists and turns of Del Monte Forest. The sound even more than the sight of the races stays with me; the tall pine trees seemed to act like megaphones, increasing the volume with their echoes. I also remember wandering, bedazzled, among the many fantastic cars displayed on the lawn of the Del Monte Lodge, now The Lodge at Pebble Beach, and wishing more than a few were mine. I was a young teenager at the time, and teenage experiences and desires tend to stick with you.

I return to the Pebble Beach Concours d'Elegance again and again because it has become a part of me—just as it is a part of many people. In fact, since 1952, I think I have missed only two or three years, while serving in the military. When the event celebrated its thirtieth birthday, in 1980, I wrote and published *Pebble Beach, A Matter of Style,* a book about its early history. For much of the last two decades I have also had the honor of serving regularly as one of its class judges.

Of course, I have participated in many other automotive events as well. In my twenties, I took part in numerous sports car and formula junior races, and over the ensuing decades, I have participated in and helped to organize many concours, tours, and rallies. I am particularly active in the Ferrari Club of America; I have served as its national secretary, also as concours chairman of its 1994 International Meeting, and frequently as judge at the national level. Cars and car people simply delight me. I have written numerous articles and almost everything I write is about cars.

Through the happenstance of birth, I was also exposed to the world of art from a very young age, and I have grown to treasure it. There was an original print in our house of the French poster *Le Divan Japonais* created by Henri de Toulouse-Lautrec in 1893. Its colors and contrasts, its style and its mystery stay with me. It was an epic work and I never understood it entirely. But there is no doubt that seeing that work daily in my youth was the early source of inspiration that led to this very book!

While spending my early summers in Monterey, I also had the opportunity to meet and know and gain inspiration from many of the artists that composed the "Carmel School of Art"—luminaries such as photographers Ansel Adams and brothers Cole and Brett Weston, and renowned watercolor artist Donald Teague.

I am not an artist myself, but I take pleasure in collecting artwork that inspires me. My collection includes both sculptures and paintings, and as you might imagine, much of it celebrates the automobiles from the eras that interest me.

Included in my collection are a substantial number of automotive posters. I kept the posters from all the early Pebble Beach Road Race and Pebble Beach Concours d'Elegance events that I attended, and then I just added to their number over the years. Initially, I did not think of these posters as artwork; they were just pictures of things that I wanted to remember. I tacked them up on my college room walls. Now I regret those tack holes, of course.

This book has afforded me the opportunity to study these posters in depth and to get to know the artists that created them. It has also given me the chance to revisit the history of and learn even more about an event that I revere. For this I am grateful.

By day, in truth, I live by numbers; I am an investment counselor, but it is family and friends and my many passions that sustain me. And I'm happy to share those passions with you.

Acknowledgments

No single person creates a book like this; it is the result of the dreams and the labor of many individuals.

The Pebble Beach Concours d'Elegance is at the heart of this book, and I first want to thank the many people who have made it the event that it is—an event that has endured for fifty-three years and has come to be recognized as the premier event of its type in the world. People and their visions, and the physical and emotional energy they put forth, are what make an event soar, and from its start to the present, the Concours has been well guided.

The initial Pebble Beach Concours d'Elegance was an offshoot of the first Pebble Beach Road Race, and the primary visionaries and organizers of the race were Sterling Edwards, Bill Breeze, and the San Francisco Region of the Sports Car Club of America (SCCA). John B. Morse, then President of Del Monte Properties Company, which is now Pebble Beach Company, deserves credit for agreeing to host the race at Pebble Beach, and Kay and Kjell Qvale of British Motor Car Corporation in San Francisco worked hard to pull it off. The addition of the Concours came about largely through the efforts of two people: local Pebble Beach resident Alton Walker, an avid car collector who served as the first Concours Chairman, and Gwenn Graham, head of publicity for Del Monte Properties Company. I had the pleasure during my teen years of assisting Walker on a number of restorations, including two Silver Ghost Playboy Roadsters, a Phantom II Henley Roadster, and a 1913 London to Edinburgh Tourer. Gwenn Graham's organizational talents were exceptional, and she and her team of assistants shepherded the Concours through its first eighteen years. After her death, first Carol Rissel, then Robert Campbell, and more recently Karen Hunter and Sandra Kasky guided the Concours on behalf of the company. In 1992, Sandra moved to a consulting role with the company so she could become the event's first full-time Executive Director.

The Pebble Beach Concours, as we know it today, would not exist without the dynamic duo of Lorin Tryon and Jules "J." Heumann, who served as Co-Chairmen of the event from 1972 until Lorin's death in early 1999. Their automotive knowledge, their talent as organizers, and their demanding standards brought the Concours to the premier status it now enjoys. Today, J. Heumann is Chairman Emeritus, and the future of the event is in the capable hands of two new Co-Chairmen, Glenn Mounger and Sandra Kasky, and Chief Judge Ed Gilbertson.

The many individuals that volunteer their services on behalf of the Concours are legion, and they also deserve mention. Representatives of Concours charities, like Rody Holt, James Glaser, and Richard Murnighan, have devoted numerous hours to this event, and many individuals, such as Chris Bock, Charles Downes, and Paul Woudenberg, have played key roles on a long-standing basis. I also want to acknowledge the many people who have gone to the effort and expense of restoring and showing their collector cars, and the qualified judges who determine the outcome of each competition.

As they say in real estate circles, the most important three elements in a site are location, location, and location. Well, thanks to Pebble Beach Company, the Pebble Beach Concours d'Elegance is held on what many consider to be the most perfect meeting of land and sea in the world—the eighteenth fairway of Pebble Beach Golf Links.

Now to the specific credits to be given for this book:

Credit goes first and foremost to the poster artists, of course. Just over two dozen artists created the dynamic images on the posters that have translated the Pebble Beach Concours d'Elegance to the world over the past fifty-three years. While these individuals are from varied backgrounds, they share a binding passion for what they do and how they do it.

I salute each and every one of these artists for their contributions. I also thank them for agreeing to be interviewed by me, for being willing to share their stories and their artistic vision in the pages of this book.

Extra thanks go to Ken Eberts, longtime president of the Automotive Fine Arts Society (AFAS). Ken was one of the first artists that I interviewed, and he helped me to better understand the significance of the automotive fine arts movement.

The Carmel Art Association and the Monterey Public Library were prompt and attentive to my many requests for information, particularly regarding those poster artists who are deceased.

Kandace Hawkinson, with whom I have had the pleasure of working on previous occasions, applied her considerable editorial skills to the entire content of this book. She is a true pro.

My longtime friend Charles W. Queener lent his deft hand to the layout of these pages, and the Lavenham Press brought this book to fruition, meshing text and design onto paper.

Publishers Glyn Morris and Martin Button of Dalton Watson Fine Books have my respect and admiration for their decision to publish this book.

Despite the efforts of all of these individuals, this book might not have seen the light of day, but for strong support from two key sources:

Ford Motor Company stepped forward in a major way, on the occasion of its centennial, helping to underwrite a good portion of the cost that is incurred in creating a fine press book of the highest quality. Its support ensured that we could create the book we wanted to create—a book with both substance and style. Ford's contribution to automotive art is to be lauded.

Don Williams of the Blackhawk Collection had the foresight, years ago, to preserve and catalog all of the Pebble Beach Concours poster art. His archive of posters and transparencies served as the foundation for the posters depicted in this book. Don has given this project his enthusiastic support, and he, too, has provided financial backing.

On a personal note, I have dedicated this book to my parents, Arthur Coghlan Devlin and Dorothy Eleanor Valentine Devlin—two unique individuals with well-developed personalities who lovingly nurtured their four children, of which I am the third born. My parents encouraged each of us to set our own sails, to develop the individual interests that would lead us to become what we wanted to be. They blended traditional ethics and respect for others with a progressive outlook that always asked the question "Why not?" rather than "Why?" Both of my parents have now departed from this world, but they have left behind a legacy of service to the community and many friends who dearly miss their stimulating company.

Final credit goes to my wife Elizabeth Davis Devlin for her day-in-and-day-out, very levelheaded assistance with communications to and from editors, artists and all the other participants. She was also my ongoing support. Thank you Betsy!

Robert T. Devlin

A Brief History: The Pebble Beach Concours d'Elegance and its Posters

■ AUTOMOBILES WERE BORN OF DREAMS, AND TO THIS DAY, THEY INHABIT OUR VISIONS. THEY NOT ONLY transport us to new places, they deliver us to the realm of new possibilities. They fuel our hopes. They serve as inspiration. The automobile is muse to us all.

The Automobile and the Early Concours d'Elegance

It was back in the mid-1880s that men of ingenuity first placed internal combustion engines in various wheeled contraptions, crafting the earliest motorized vehicles. Gottlieb Daimler created the first motorcycle in 1885, Karl Benz introduced a three-wheel vehicle the following January, and before summer's end the first four-wheel horseless carriage, another Daimler creation, had been developed.

These and other early automobiles were curiosities for the most part; few people could build or afford to buy them. Those who could simply took pleasure in them. Quite often these pleasurable pursuits involved a bit of friendly competition—some owners sought to prove their car's speed while others sought to exhibit its craftsmanship and beauty. Thus motor sport and the concours d'elegance were born in tandem. The earliest concours d'elegance were just informal parades of automobiles down popular boulevards, but these events quickly became more organized, particularly in France, where they soon evolved into heated contests, with winners and prizes. Whether race or concours, early automotive events drew the curious from near and far.

The automobile was also included in several general exhibitions. It was a heady time for mankind as the nineteenth century turned into the twentieth; a number of major developments were taking place in the field of transportation, and there were numerous expositions to celebrate these achievements. Ships and trains were moving faster, and planes were about to take to the air. All would transport the masses on strict schedules. But it was only the automobile that would transport individuals wherever and whenever they desired.

Henry Ford is often credited with putting the world on wheels. His first automotive creation, a Quadricycle, was not introduced until 1896—a full decade after the earliest motorized vehicles—but it was Ford who determined to build a car that many people could afford. After he founded Ford Motor Company in 1903, the Model T Roadster debuted in 1908 with a price tag of $825, less than a third of many competing models, and its price actually declined as Ford's moving assembly line was introduced and production became more efficient. By the end of its run, in 1927, over 15 million Model Ts were on the road. Cars were no longer mere curiosities; they were an affordable way for individuals to travel from one place to another on their own schedule.

Races and concours continued, of course. Well-heeled individuals still wanted the best cars that money could buy, and certain manufacturers and select coachbuilding firms were ready to oblige them. For a hefty fee, they designed and built cars that were tailored to suit a client's specific tastes and desires. Often individuals bought the latest chassis from the marque they preferred and then sent it to their favorite coachbuilder to be bodied. Custom coachwork reached its zenith in the late 1920s and the 1930s—an era now revered by connoisseurs of automotive style. The latest designs often debuted at the concours d'elegance, as did the latest couture fashions.

War put an end to the races and the concours—at least for a time.

World War I had disrupted the early growth of the automotive industry, particularly in Europe, and the Great Depression had troubled many American manufacturers. But World War II was absolutely devastating for the industry as a whole. Raw materials were diverted and many factories were retooled to produce the weapons of war. Some plants were physically destroyed. Financial losses took their toll on other manufacturers. Many small custom coachbuilders simply folded; coachbuilding would never resume on the same scale.

Of course, the automotive industry as a whole would survive—and prosper. And the attendant competition would too.

The Rise of the Pebble Beach Concours d'Elegance

In postwar America there was renewed appreciation for all things European. It was no longer simply "the old country" that waves of immigrants had abandoned; it was land and heritage and culture that Americans had fought hard to help save. Jaguars and MGs and other cars of European origin were suddenly in vogue. And their owners wanted to race them as the Europeans did—on public roads as well as private tracks.

In the fall of 1950, the leaders of the San Francisco Region of the Sports Car Club of America determined to host the first real "European style" road race on the West Coast of the United States. The venue they selected was a posh resort on the Monterey Peninsula of California that regularly hosted an elite mix of the socially recognized, rich and royal. Moreover, the place was widely known for its scenic 17-Mile Drive that wound along the Pacific Coast and through nearby forests.

Plans for the first Pebble Beach Road Race were rapidly set in motion. At the eleventh hour, organizers decided to add a concours d'elegance to the race, to give it a touch of class. Concours cars would gather near what is now the Beach and Tennis Club at Pebble Beach Resorts, and they would parade up to the Race's opening straightaway, giving spectators a glimpse of automotive beauty before they witnessed hours of speed and power.

Alton Walker, a resident of Pebble Beach, served as Chairman of the first Pebble Beach Concours d'Elegance. Walker had long owned the Shell Oil and Gasoline dealership at the Monterey Airport, and he was among the first to realize that visiting celebrities arriving by air would need ground transportation. Walker had filled that need by rescuing and leasing several antique, vintage, and other prewar automobiles. By 1950, he owned an amazing assortment of such cars, and selected examples from his collection constituted the bulk of the older cars entered in the first Pebble Beach Concours d'Elegance. By far, however, the majority of entries—and winners—in the first several Concours were current British sedans and sports cars.

In its third year, in 1952, the Pebble Beach Concours truly became an entity of its own; it preceded the Race by a day and Concours entries no longer paraded down the Race straightaway. Instead, they posed elegantly on the swath of green grass that has long since become the event's scenic home—the wide lush lawn that runs from what is now The Lodge at Pebble Beach down to the eighteenth green of Pebble Beach Golf Links and the edge of Carmel Bay. Spectators could stroll casually among the Concours entries, relishing their beauty in a relaxed and social setting.

Cars with custom coachwork soon began to appear among Concours entries, but at least initially, their individuality was not appreciated. The 1953 entries included a remarkable Ferrari 212 by Vignale, but Best of Show was awarded instead to an Austin-Healey 100! Judging was admittedly subjective in the Concours' early years; local personalities and socialites with little automotive knowledge simply pooled their good taste and pronounced their collective choice as the winner.

The year 1955 helped everyone to better define what was desired on the field. After heated debate among the judges, Phil Hill's 1931 Pierce Arrow 41 Le Baron Convertible Town Cabriolet won Best of Show. This marked the first time that the general predilection for "new" over "old" did not hold. The car's classic style was recognized despite its age. Over time, the term *classic* would increasingly be used to refer specifically to those prewar cars created during the heyday of the custom coachbuilders from the mid-1920s through the 1930s, and such cars would actually come to be preferred at the Concours.

Race and Concours continued to be paired in one automotive weekend until 1956 when one of the race drivers was killed in an accident and the race subsequently moved elsewhere. Thereafter, the Concours struggled somewhat for direction, though it gained some purpose in 1961 when it began to benefit a local charity, the Community Hospital Auxiliary. Over the years, its beneficiaries have changed, but it has always remained a charitable endeavor.

The year 1972 was a watershed for the Concours. Two ardent car enthusiasts, Lorin Tryon and Jules "J." Heumann, stepped up to serve as Co-Chairmen, and they immediately instituted several changes that would take the show from local benefit to world-class event: two new panels of expert judges were established, and they were asked to follow specific guidelines in making their decisions; class categories were revised, affirming the show's strong preference for prewar classics; and entries were limited to only the most spectacular cars.

In 1974, with approval from Concours officials, the first Monterey Historic Automobile Races took place at Laguna Seca Raceway just prior to the Concours. Over the years, the two events would continue to be held concurrently, often featuring the same marque. Many other automotive events have also been

added to the mix. More recently, 1998 witnessed the debut of the Pebble Beach Tour d'Elegance, a driving event for Concours entries. The days leading up to the Concours now offer enthusiasts an automotive feast.

From quite early in its history, the Concours had often featured certain marques and special exhibits, adding a pinch of spice to its regular competition classes. There was a special class for MGs the very first year. Two Mexican Road Race winners were exhibited in 1953. And the marques Rolls-Royce and Bentley had been featured—and favored—through much of the late 1950s and 1960s. Over time, the featured marques and exhibits would become increasingly important, setting the tone for a given year. Delage and Duesenberg, Ferrari and Ford, Maybach and Mercedes, Hispano-Suiza and Isotta Fraschini would all have their day. In more recent years, there have even been some rather unexpected delights, like the presence of hot rods, microcars and bare chassis on the field.

It was the year 1985 that affirmed the premier status of the Pebble Beach Concours d'Elegance among automotive events worldwide. The year's featured marque was Bugatti, and after much negotiating, J. and Lorin and a host of the Concours' supporters arranged for all six of Ettore Bugatti's masterworks, his Bugatti Royales, to be united at Pebble Beach. That union was a feat never previously accomplished and one unlikely to be repeated.

Tryon and Heumann eventually served for 28 years as Co-Chairmen. Sadly, Lorin died in 1999, just a year before the Pebble Beach Concours d'Elegance celebrated its fiftieth anniversary. The Concours is now under the fine leadership of Co-Chairmen Glenn Mounger and Sandra Kasky.

Automotive Art and the Pebble Beach Concours d'Elegance Posters

The concours d'elegance has always focused on the automobile as an art object, but the automobile has long been the subject of art as well.

As soon as the first automobiles were created and sold, they were featured in advertisements, brochures, and catalogs. Such items were not considered art at the time; they were simply publicity materials. Looking back, however, these items were often artistically drawn, they were produced with a certain attention to quality, and today they have value to those who treasure the automobile.

Similarly, there were advertisements for the many early events that involved the automobile—for expositions and races and concours d'elegance. These advertisements generally took the form of posters. At least initially, posters, like other advertisements, were thought to have no residual, or lasting, value. But over time that perception would change.

Posters were still the primary means for announcing and promoting events when the first Pebble Beach Road Race and Pebble Beach Concours d'Elegance were held in 1950, and indeed a poster was created for the occasion. But that poster focused solely on the Race, not mentioning the Concours at all. The same held true when the events were repeated the following year. In 1952, Race organizers finally acknowledged the Concours' growing importance and accorded it a brief mention. It would not receive more than that until the Race and the Concours separated a few years later. The first poster created to advertise the Concours itself appeared in 1958. The Concours was on shaky ground in the first few years after its separation from the Race; it was not held in 1960, and posters have not been found for the Concours in 1961 or 1962. But posters have been created for every Pebble Beach Concours since 1963.

These posters vary dramatically in the mediums used, their style and vision, and the technology involved in their creation and printing, but all clearly celebrate the automobile.

The first Race poster featured an etched image and type, and was printed in just one color. The next several Race and Concours posters were done in what is now called "boxing style," which was common to posters from the 1940s well into the 1960s; these posters featured black-and-white photographs with block or boxed textual graphics. In addition to black, they utilized one additional color at most. All of these early posters were printed on medium-weight cardboard stock, and they were large, but not oversized, measuring roughly 11 by 14 inches. A few fans of the Race and Concours saved these posters as mementos, but they were never viewed as anything more than that.

The year 1966 marked a dramatic change in the Concours posters. Cartoonist supreme Eldon Dedini, a regular contributor to *Esquire, The New Yorker* and *Playboy* magazines, agreed to create that year's poster, and he continued to do so for eight consecutive years. His vivid, often fantastic images served the Concours well, drawing people to the event even while it struggled to find its footing and its focus.

Dedini brought his knowledge of art history, especially poster history, to his work. His first poster, for example, featured a rough stark image and hand lettering that echoed the works of the German Jugendstil artists of the late nineteenth century. His second poster was a tribute to "Moulin Rouge–La Goulue," a poster by famous French artist Henri de Toulouse-Lautrec that is now viewed as a revolutionary piece of artwork. Later Dedini posters translated popular and contemporary art movements. Dedini also researched early automotive art; he bought old automotive brochures, catalogs, and books, culling through them to find themes and images he could replicate.

Dedini's images added real value to the Concours posters; he had a following as an artist, and people collected his work. The posters were still intended primarily as publicity pieces, but extra copies of Dedini's posters were sold directly to the public, and much of Dedini's original artwork was also auctioned off. Dedini donated his work, and all the proceeds from these poster sales and auctions went directly to Concours charities. This set a precedent, and to this day, a substantial portion of the sales from Concours posters and artwork continues to go to Concours charities.

All of the posters Dedini created in this period were serigraphs; they were original silk screen prints with each color printed individually on a separate run through the press.

In 1974, a montage of photo images was used again, this time with color overlays by graphic artist Colden Whitman. From 1975 to 1985, Concours posters featured the artwork of many different local artists, several of whom were also car enthusiasts. Depictions of cars on the posters were increasingly important; in fact these artists were often asked to emphasize a specific marque or car, in accord with the Concours' featured marques and exhibits. Some of these posters were printed on four-color presses, and a few of them made use of newer metallic inks. The posters also grew to standard poster size and they were printed on regular poster paper. As was true for posters in general, the role of the Concours poster was diminishing as a publicity tool, but its value as treasured memento and as artwork in its own right was on the rise.

There has long been debate over what constitutes *fine art,* in terms of appropriate mediums, styles, and subjects. In the latter half of the twentieth century, several key automotive artists argued with increasing fervor that automobiles were a very suitable subject for fine art. In 1983, six artists banded together to form the Automotive Fine Arts Society (AFAS) to promote and exhibit such artwork. Just three years later, the Pebble Beach Concours d'Elegance was proud to host a major exhibition of automotive fine art. Deemed an immediate success, the exhibit was quickly repeated, and it is now a much-anticipated part of the Concours.

In the intervening years, Concours posters have also shifted from featuring graphic art to fine art. Ken Eberts, AFAS president, was selected to design the 1986 Concours poster, and he served as poster artist again in 1987, 1988, 1994, and 2003. He also painted the first poster for the Pebble Beach Tour d'Elegance. Other members of the AFAS have created Concours and Tour posters as well. In fact, AFAS members have created all but two of the Concours and Tour posters from 1986 through 2003. Eldon Dedini returned as poster artist in 1990 when the Concours celebrated its fortieth anniversary. And on the occasion of its fiftieth anniversary, the Concours commissioned two posters—one by AFAS artist John Francis Marsh depicting the Concours' history, and another by noted photographer Ron Kimball showing the year's featured marque. The latter poster hearkens back to the early posters that used photographs, but it was created with the latest computer technology.

Seen together, the Pebble Beach Concours d'Elegance posters allow viewers to relive the amazing history of the world's top automotive event and they also offer insight into the growth of automotive art.

We hope you enjoy them.

Posters from the Pebble Beach Concours d'Elegance 1950–2003

1950 John Courtney Sandefur

■ THE INAUGURAL PEBBLE BEACH CONCOURS D'ELEGANCE, HELD ON NOVEMBER 5, 1950, WAS, IN TRUTH, AN aperitif—a stylish start to that day's automotive feast. The first Pebble Beach Concours was a prelude to the first Pebble Beach Road Race. The events remained paired through most of the decade.

Shortly after 11 A.M. on that Sunday in 1950, a few dozen cars—some antiques, some classics, and several current models—paraded briefly before spectators. By noon, race cars were rushing through Del Monte Forest.

Press releases and subsequent press reports for the paired events focused almost exclusively on the Road Race, as did the poster created to advertise the occasion. That poster was designed by respected commercial artist John Courtney Sandefur, who had moved to the Monterey, California, area just two years earlier.

Born in Alexandria, Indiana, in 1893, Sandefur studied at both the Herron School of Art in Indianapolis and the Art Institute of Chicago, and he was a member of the Chicago Society of Etchers. In 1930 he moved to Los Angeles, and in 1948 he headed up the coast to Pacific Grove, where he resided until his death in 1971. His later work attests to his love of the area; his intricate etchings of Monterey scenes appeared on a series of popular greeting cards.

Sandefur's work is included in the National Museum of American Art in Washington, D.C., and his signed engravings have sold well at auction.

The 1950 poster exhibits Sandefur's attention to fine detail. On it, he captures the side profile of the recently introduced Jaguar XK120 roadster—the standard model without modified engine and wire wheels. He was perhaps prescient in this selection because a Jaguar XK120, driven by Phil Hill, went on to win the first Pebble Beach Road Race, and Jaguars also won three of the first five Pebble Beach Concours. More likely, of course, Sandefur chose to depict an XK120 simply because it then held the world speed record (of more than 132 mph) for a production car. In any case, the Jaguar on the poster is in race trim, with V-shaped windshield removed. The helmeted driver with goggles is shown executing a right-hand turn, and the trail of dust behind the car and the subtle lines of motion on the Jaguar allude to the exhilarating speed that spectators will experience at the races.

The car's location in the poster is a bit deceptive. Race organizers had initially planned a racing circuit that would utilize portions of famed 17-Mile Drive at Pebble Beach, so Sandefur selected a scenic oceanfront portion of the drive near Bird Rock as his backdrop. But the racing circuit was changed at the last moment, at the request of local residents, and racers never passed that spot.

The artist obviously did the upper lettering on the poster. The words "Road Race" have prominence and character, with speed lines, like those on the Jaguar, trailing every letter. Long legs on both Rs directly link text with image.

Note that the poster text also emphasizes the availability of free parking—and an entry fee of just one dollar!

The artist's signature appears in the roots of a stylized cypress in the upper right corner. The original poster measures 11 by 14 inches and is printed on medium-weight cardboard stock.

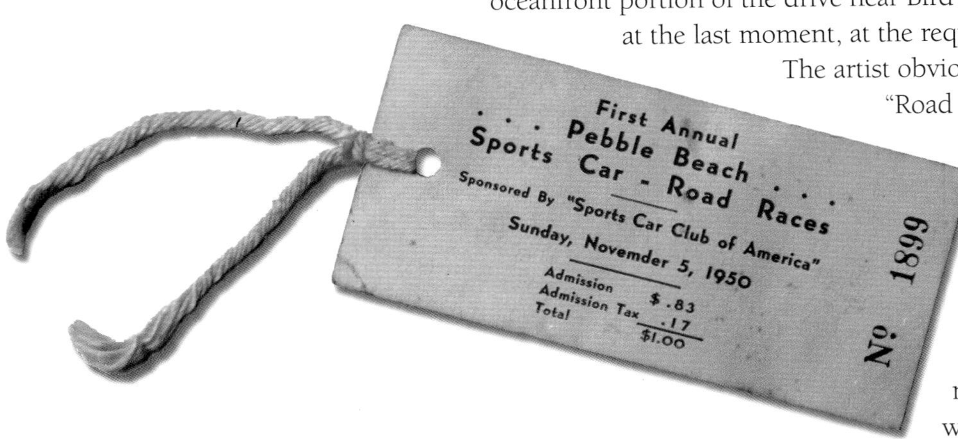

PEBBLE BEACH

Nov. 5th, 1950

•

Four Races

THRILLING EUROPEAN STYLE
ROAD RACE FEATURING
THE WORLDS FASTEST
SPORTS CARS

FIRST RACE 12:00 NOON

SPONSORED BY SPORTS CAR CLUB OF AMERICA

Tickets $1.00 Free Parking

1951 Julian P. Graham

Graphic art by Colden Whitman

■ PUBLICITY WAS CRUCIAL TO THE EARLY SUCCESS OF THE PEBBLE BEACH ROAD RACE AND THE PEBBLE BEACH Concours d'Elegance, and posters played a key role in local publicity efforts. Posters were advertisements—not treasured mementos. The goal was to place them in store windows.

As expected, the posters listed pertinent information, like dates, times and locations. They also often included a bit of explanation. Road racing was still relatively new to the United States in the 1950s, and early posters for the Pebble Beach event described it as a "Thrilling European Style Road Race Featuring the World's Fastest Sports Cars." Better yet, the posters offered an enticing glimpse of the excitement people might witness. Striking black-and-white photographs were featured on all but one of the posters created from 1951 to 1965, and most of these photographs were the work of Julian P. "Spike" Graham. Graham served as the official photographer at many major Pebble Beach events from 1924 until his death in 1963.

Born in Washington, D.C., in 1886, Graham initially sought a career in semipro baseball, earning the nickname "Spike." Eventually, at his family's urging, he shifted his focus. He also headed West.

Once in Monterey, Graham worked initially out of the old Hotel Del Monte, which was at that time the crown jewel of Del Monte Properties Company—now Pebble Beach Company. He relocated to a studio adjacent to Del Monte Lodge—now The Lodge at Pebble Beach—in 1944.

After the conclusion of World War II, the resort's reputation and its calendar of events grew rapidly. Pebble Beach drew presidents, kings and queens, movie stars, and a multitude of sports personalities, and Graham was there to photograph them all. His photographs were featured in a wide range of publications, including *Life, Time, Vogue, Harper's Bazaar,* and *National Geographic*.

The photograph featured on the 1951 poster was taken at the first Pebble Beach Road Race in 1950. The backdrop is a dramatic view of the towering Monterey pines of Del Monte Forest. Small whiffs of fog hover in the canopy, but it is the action at the base of the trees that draws the eye. Sterling Edwards in his Ford-powered 1950 Edwards R-26 Special Sport Roadster is seen leading the first lap of the Del Monte Trophy race—for cars between 1,500 and 3,000 cc. On his heels exiting turn two of the racing circuit are a pair of modified MG TCs and the BMW 328 of Joseph Esherick. Edwards, who founded the Road Race, won the Del Monte Trophy, though he lost the final race of the day, the Pebble Beach Cup, to Phil Hill. His Edwards R-26 also won Best of Show at the first Concours.

Note the string of flags at an elevated level between the trees; these flags warned drivers that they were entering a no-passing zone. Also note the hay bales stacked two-high to the outside and leading into the turn; these bales marked a long drainage ditch that paralleled the track. Organizers for the 1951 race said that "more than 50 tons of baled hay" had been secured to guard tough turns and too near trees, and the *Monterey Peninsula Herald* reported that cars would often "hit these bales . . . bounce off, and continue the race with only a dent in the side." But eventually such safety precautions would prove inadequate.

Overlaying the upper half of the 1951 poster is rich red text, designed by local graphic artist Colden Whitman. The Concours is not mentioned this year, but in ensuing years, it will be.

As in its first year, the 1951 Concours was held immediately prior to the Road Race; cars were exhibited and judged near what is now the Beach and Tennis Club beginning at 10 A.M., and then they paraded around the racing circuit. The races began promptly at noon. Tickets for the paired events were $1.50.

The original 1951 poster measures 11 by 14 inches and is printed on medium-weight cardboard stock.

2nd Annual Pebble Beach Classic
ROAD RACE
MAY 27th, 1951
THREE RACES
THRILLING EUROPEAN STYLE ROAD RACE
FEATURING THE WORLD'S FASTEST
SPORTS CARS
FIRST RACE 12:00 NOON
SPONSORED BY THE SPORTS CAR CLUB OF AMERICA
TICKETS $1.50
FREE PARKING

1952 Julian P. Graham

Graphic art by Colden Whitman

■ IN ITS THIRD YEAR, THE PEBBLE BEACH CONCOURS D'ELEGANCE GAINED DEFINITION. IT SEPARATED EVER SO slightly from the Pebble Beach Road Race, moving to precede it by a day. More importantly, it moved from field and racecourse to the lawn of The Lodge at Pebble Beach—the magnificent setting that soon became its hallmark.

Recognizing the Concours' growing importance, organizers added specific mention of it to all 1952 print advertisements for what had become a full automotive weekend. On the 1952 poster, this first mention appears almost at center. The Road Race gets top billing, of course, and the relative weight of the type—its size and boldness—also affords that event more prominence.

The photograph on the 1952 poster first appeared on the cover of the official program distributed at the 1951 Road Race and Concours. Perhaps the photograph was shot when the events were first paired in November 1950. It may even predate that first pairing. The photograph distinctly echoes the action and setting of the etching used on the 1950 program and poster. When viewed together, this photograph seems to bring that etching to life. So one may have served as model for the other.

This photograph is the work of Julian P. Graham, who served as the official photographer at Pebble Beach for nearly four decades. Graham is also previously credited with the photograph used on the 1951 poster, and his work would continue to be featured on posters for many years to come.

Graham knew the whole of Pebble Beach, angle by angle, and he favored certain spots for his posed publicity shots—spots where land met water and he could capture the beauty of that meeting. He chose Pescadero Point, located on 17-Mile Drive just one half mile west of The Lodge, as the location for the publicity photo used on the 1952 poster.

In the background of this photo, Graham carefully frames a view to the southeast—a view looking back across the water of Carmel Bay to the long expanse of white sand that is Carmel Beach, resting at the foot of rising coastal headlands. In the foreground, he frames his subject with cypress trees.

The subject is the black 1950 Jaguar XK120 then owned by William N. "Bill" Breeze, a regional official for the Sports Car Club of America and a member of the race's organizing committee. The car is distinguished by its rear fender skirts. Another Jaguar XK120—a 1952 Fixed Head Coupé owned by Glen Sorey—would take the Concours' top prize in 1952.

Note that the photograph shows Breeze driving on the shoulder of the wrong side of the road, kicking up dust. Most likely, Graham asked Breeze to do this to give the photograph an element of action. To safely obtain this shot, Graham must have had some assistance stopping traffic, at least briefly, along 17-Mile Drive.

The vertical nature of this photograph, like that used on the 1951 poster, provides ample upper space for text. Local graphic artist Colden Whitman places much of that text in accord with his original 1951 design. One new font is introduced, and some text shifts to the left to make room for the added mention of the Concours. The most dramatic change is the text's vibrant yellow color.

The small text at bottom notes that the price of a ticket to the Road Races is now $2.00. At least tax is included!

The original poster measures 11 by 13¾ inches and is printed on medium-weight cardboard stock.

Pebble Beach Sports Car
ROAD RACE
APRIL 20, 1952
Three Races--
Thrilling European Style
Featuring World's Fastest
Sports Cars
CONCOURS D'ELEGANCE
Saturday, April 19
1:00 to 5:00
FIRST RACE 12:00 NOON
SPONSORED BY THE SPORTS CAR CLUB OF AMERICA
TICKETS $2.00 (Tax Included)
FREE PARKING

1953 Julian P. Graham
Graphic art by Colden Whitman

■ Throughout the early years of the Pebble Beach Concours d'Elegance, many of its spectators and even some key participants had difficulty describing the event. Any single definition failed. The Concours was initially part parade, part beauty pageant, part serious competition, and part social mixer. It was even—to be quite honest—part showroom and sales floor for several new car dealers.

Despite the confusion, the organizers of the 1953 Concours decided to add yet another facet to the event—that of a special exhibition. The first exhibition was small, consisting of just two winning cars from the Carrera Panamericana (the Mexican Road Race), held the previous fall. But the crowd enjoyed it and the press praised the added feature. Over time, such displays would multiply.

The 1953 poster advertising the Road Race and Concours had new facets, too. Local graphic artist Colden Whitman decided to do more than just place text on top of a photograph, as he had done in 1951 and 1952. The 1953 poster exhibits one of his earliest efforts to crop a photograph irregularly, and then pair it with both text and bold color blocks. Whitman traced an intricate edge on the photo, eliminating more than a third of the original image. Then he filled the gaping hole with a rich teal blue. Key text reversed out of that blue in eye-popping white, while less important descriptive phrases ran in basic black. On the lower fifth of the final poster, the opposite color scheme was used: an off-white horizontal band ran across the page, with key text in teal blue. The resulting poster had a clean, contemporary look.

The 1953 poster did continue tradition in one key sense: the photograph that Whitman cropped was again a black-and-white image by Julian P. Graham, the official photographer at Pebble Beach.

The photograph captures a scene from the feature race in 1952. Phil Hill is shown at the wheel of the rare right-hand-drive Jaguar XK120 LT-3—and just three such cars were built! Hastings Harcourt follows in a Baldwin Mercury Special. Both men are navigating the left dogleg that leads into the final straightaway and pit area. Hill's car eventually overheated, he had to stop for water, and he finished fifth just behind Harcourt, while Bill Pollack, driving a Cadillac Allard J-2, garnered his second consecutive win.

In 1953, Hill returned to win the feature race, driving a Ferrari 250 MM. Perhaps the 1953 poster served as inspiration.

The original 1953 poster measures 11 by 14 inches and is printed on medium-weight cardboard stock.

FIRST RACE 1:00 P. M.

Tickets $2.00 (tax included)

Free Parking

CONCOURS D'ELEGANCE

Saturday April 18

1:00 to 5:00

SPONSORED BY THE SPORTS CAR CLUB OF AMERICA

1954 Colden Whitman

Photography by Julian P. Graham

■ Working on his fourth consecutive poster for the Pebble Beach Road Race and Concours d'Elegance, graphic artist Colden Whitman came into his own. Rather than simply pasting up photograph, color block, and text, he added his own illustration to the equation, creating a unique work of art.

Colden Whitman was born in St. Louis, Missouri, in 1922, but his family moved to Carmel while he was still a young boy, and he has lived in the area most of his life. Immediately out of high school, during World War II, Whitman served for three years in the Pacific with a U.S. Army engineering unit. Upon his return, he briefly attended Washington University in St. Louis and joined the D'Arcy Advertising Agency. He soon returned to Carmel to start his own advertising agency, working as a graphic artist. In addition to his work for the Pebble Beach Road Race and Concours d'Elegance, he has worked on printed materials for the Monterey Jazz Festival, the Monterey Wine Festival, the Bing Crosby National Pro-Am, and the AT&T Pebble Beach National Pro-Am. Now retired, he enjoys painting watercolors.

A modest man, Whitman often downplays his role in the creative process; he generally refers to the photographs or illustrations that he used on posters as "the artwork" and his own contributions as mere graphic overlay. But that distinction doesn't hold true for the work he did on the 1954 poster.

As in previous years, Whitman has used a race photograph taken by Julian P. Graham as the focus of the poster.

In this case, the photograph dates back to the 1952 Pebble Beach Trophy race for unsupercharged cars up to 1,500 cc. Two Roger Barlow Simca 8 Specials are seen navigating hairpin turn number four, which wraps tightly around the base of a large pine tree. These race cars were among the first built specifically to take on the modified production cars, and they had won previous races up and down the coast. In this case, car number 62 is driven by Barlow and the trailing car is driven by Bill Pringle. Barlow ultimately won the race and Pringle finished third.

Whitman cut jaggedly across this photo at its midsection, then artistically redrew the outlines of tree trunks and canopy with pen and ink. Judging from the portion of the photograph that remains, Whitman effectively removed a lot of distracting brush and dense forest, bringing more light to the page, while keeping the focus on the cars.

Red color blocks at the upper left and lower right contain text, which appears in black and white. Reference to the Concours is quite prominent. Note, too, that proceeds from the Race are now benefiting the American Cancer Society. In future years the Concours would also support many charitable endeavors.

Whitman's signature appears on the left side, between the photograph and the upper left text block.

The original 1954 poster measures 11 by 13½ inches and is printed on medium-weight cardboard stock.

PEBBLE BEACH
SPORTS CAR
Road Race
APRIL 11 - 1954
FOUR RACES · THRILLING
EUROPEAN STYLE · FEATURING
WORLD'S FASTEST SPORTS CARS
WHITMAN
62 6
FIRST RACE 10:00 A. M.
TICKETS $2.00 - FREE PARKING
CONCOURS D'ELEGANCE
SATURDAY, APRIL 10 - 11:00 TO 5:00
SPONSORED BY THE SPORTS CAR CLUB OF AMERICA
BENEFIT OF AMERICAN CANCER SOCIETY

1955 Julian P. Graham William C. Brooks

Graphic art by Colden Whitman

■ IN THE 1950S, THE TERM *CLASSIC CAR* WAS JUST BEGINNING TO BE USED. IN THE MINDS OF MOST PEOPLE, CARS were simply old or new—and new was to be preferred.

In its first five years, the Pebble Beach Concours d'Elegance awarded its top prize to new cars without exception. But in 1955 one classic car caused spectators and judges alike to reexamine their thinking. That car was a 1931 Pierce-Arrow 41 LeBaron Convertible Town Cabriolet owned and loved, and very carefully restored, by race driver Phil Hill. After substantial debate, judges presented Hill's Pierce-Arrow with the 1955 Best of Show trophy. A new trend—a preference for classics—had begun.

Phil Hill actually recorded a double win at Pebble Beach in 1955; he drove a Ferrari 750 Monza to victory in the Road Race that same year. The Road Race was still the primary event of the Pebble Beach automotive weekend, as the 1955 poster makes clear. The poster features a race photograph taken by either Julian P. Graham or William C. Brooks. Graham was the official photographer at Pebble Beach until his death in 1963, but in his later years he shared his assignments with Brooks, who ran the camera shop at The Lodge at Pebble Beach from 1953 to 1986.

Born in Paducah, Kentucky, in 1914, William C. "Bill" Brooks served with the U.S. Army during World War II, attaining the rank of Captain, before moving to Carmel in 1945.

After doing some freelance work, he eventually paired up with Graham, and through much of the 1950s and early 1960s, the two men worked closely together. A skilled photographer from the very start, Brooks was soon functioning as a partner, often taking photographs on Graham's behalf. And when Graham died in 1963, Brooks succeeded him as the official photographer at Pebble Beach.

A quiet and unassuming man, Brooks was nonetheless quite comfortable—and more than capable—working in the company of very well-known individuals. At Pebble Beach, he photographed President Dwight D. Eisenhower, John F. Kennedy, Adlai Stevenson, the Shah of Iran, Bing Crosby, and Eleanor Roosevelt, among others. Using a Graflex camera to take large-format negatives, he would work quickly, and then, with a tip of his hat, thank his subjects and bid them adieu. The resulting portraits were superb. His landscapes were equally good, dramatically distilling the natural setting of Pebble Beach—its varied coastline and deep forest. And Brooks took great joy in capturing the moment—whether that be an event of historic importance or a passing expression of emotion.

In this photo, big-bore modified cars barrel up the hill to hairpin turn four—the slowest point on the racecourse—during one of the early laps of the 1954 Del Monte Trophy race. The photographer has situated himself on a slight rise above the track at the turn's exit so he can capture the cars as they lay down rubber and accelerate out of the turn. You can almost hear and smell the action: first there is the grinding of gears as the cars go uphill; then you hear the squeal of brakes as they try to negotiate the turn; and finally, there is the distinct smell of rubber.

The photo shows Chrysler Allard #64, driven by Carl Block, in the lead. Mercury Kurtis #105 and #130, driven respectively by Bill Stroppe and Alex Budurin, both follow. Stroppe will eventually take the lead and set a course lap record before the crankshaft of his overstressed engine fails. And in the end, Sterling Edwards, driving a Ferrari 340 MM, will win.

On top of this photograph, Colden Whitman has placed the text in bright yellow and white boxes. Two of the boxes are set at an angle, and Whitman has taken the time to add drop shadows. A checkered flag adds interest.

The original 1955 poster measures 10½ by 13¼ inches and is printed on medium-weight cardboard stock.

6th Annual
PEBBLE BEACH
Sports Car
Road Race
APRIL 17 • 1955
thrilling european style races
world's fastest sports cars
130c
105
FIRST RACE 10 A. M.
Tickets $2.00
Free Parking
CONCOURS D'ELEGANCE
Saturday, April 16 • 11:00 to 5:00
No admission charge
SPONSORED BY THE SPORTS CAR CLUB OF AMERICA
BENEFIT OF AMERICAN CANCER SOCIETY

1956 Julian P. Graham Jr.

Graphic art by Colden Whitman

A GLANCE AT THIS 1956 POSTER MAKES ONE THING CLEAR: ROAD RACING IS TO BE FEARED.

The poster features a photograph taken in 1955 when the most dangerous racecourse on the West Coast was drenched in rain, making it more dangerous still.

During the 1950s and early 1960s, several photographers worked under Julian P. Graham, including his son, Julian P. Graham Jr., who was better known as "Hooly." A 1955 issue of *Game & Gossip* gives credit to Hooly, who was born in Los Gatos, California, in 1921, for taking this photograph. It was shot from an elevated crane near the start/finish line of the Pebble Beach racing circuit during a Saturday practice session, when four cars at a time were allowed to test the course. The four cars in the foreground of the photograph are Allard #119; rebodied Jaguar LT #146, driven by Charles Fifield; Ferrari 735 Monza #26, driven by Sterling Edwards; and Triumph #111, driven by Wally Kieckhefer. In the background, barely visible through the spray, four more cars can be seen waiting to be flagged onto the course.

Lou Fageol severely damaged his twin-engined Porsche in a crash during the practice, but he himself was unharmed. The weather on Sunday was no better, and everyone exhaled with relief when the 1955 Road Races were completed without major incident.

Instead, disaster struck during fair weather in 1956. Driver Warren Frinchaboy was seriously injured during Saturday's practice, and during Sunday's feature race, Ernie McAfee was killed. The races would leave Del Monte Forest and the automotive weekend at Pebble Beach would never be the same.

The design of the 1956 poster echoes the design of previous posters, particularly the one for 1955. On top of the photograph, Colden Whitman has placed the event's title and its date in yellow and white text. A yellow color block beneath the photograph includes the remaining text. A checkered flag again adds interest.

The original 1956 poster measures 10½ by 13¼ inches and is printed on medium-weight cardboard stock.

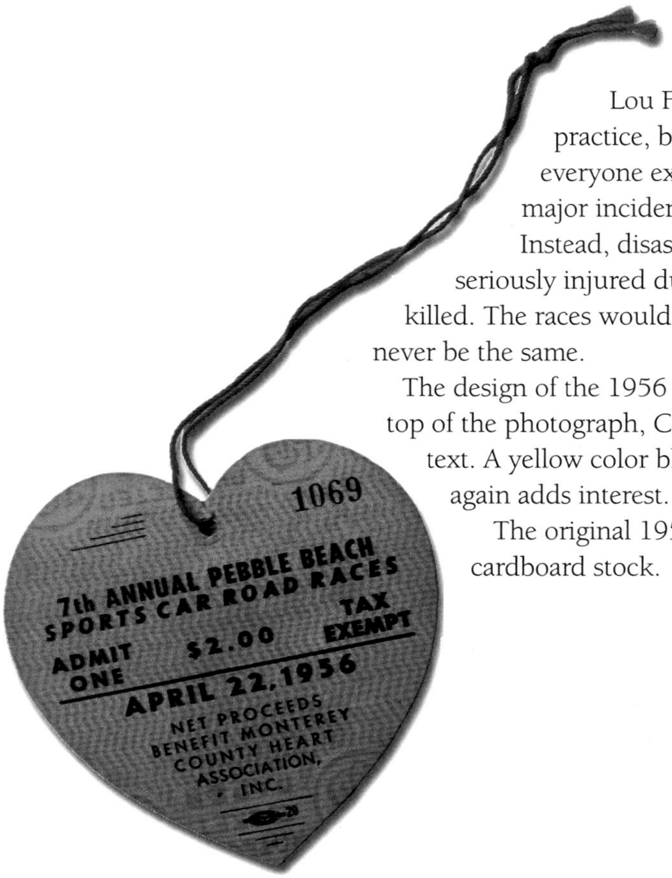

1069
7th ANNUAL PEBBLE BEACH
SPORTS CAR ROAD RACES
ADMIT ONE $2.00 TAX EXEMPT
APRIL 22, 1956
NET PROCEEDS BENEFIT MONTEREY COUNTY HEART ASSOCIATION, INC.

7TH ANNUAL

Pebble Beach

NATIONAL CHAMPIONSHIP SPORTS CAR

Road Races

APRIL 22 • 1956

FIRST RACE 10 A. M.
Tickets $2.00
Free Parking

CONCOURS D'ELEGANCE
Saturday, April 21 • 11:00 to 5:00
No admission charge

SPONSORED BY THE SPORTS CAR CLUB OF AMERICA
BENEFIT MONTEREY COUNTY HEART ASSOCIATION

1957 Artist Unknown

THE YEAR 1957 WAS ALL TRANSITION.

The tragic death of driver Ernie McAfee in 1956 brought an immediate end to road racing at Pebble Beach. Fervent enthusiasts, and their supporters, banded together to keep some semblance of racing in the area, and they more than succeeded. In the ensuing year and a half, a 1.9-mile nine-turn course was built in nearby Laguna Seca. The eighth annual Road Races, renamed the Pebble Beach at Laguna Seca National Championship Sports Car Road Races, took place there in November 1957.

The Concours was not forgotten in the turmoil. It was held concurrently, back at Pebble Beach, drawing some 10,000 spectators.

The program for the Race included a list of the 100-plus entries for the Concours. The image on the right is from the cover of that program. Despite much searching, no poster advertising either the 1957 Race or Concours has been found. It is quite possible, given the transition, that no poster was printed.

The color photograph on the program features three cars posed on a swath of green grass overlooking the Golden Gate Bridge in San Francisco. The sun is shining from the southwest, so the photo was perhaps taken on an afternoon in spring.

The cars are all current-issue Jaguars, believed to have been supplied for the photograph by British Motor Car Distributors, owned by Kjell and Kay Qvale, who had been involved in importing British motorcars since the late 1940s. They had helped to organize the original Race and Concours in 1950, and they were very faithful supporters of both events. In fact, Kjell had been involved specifically in creating and distributing the early Race programs, and he often advertised on the inside front cover.

In the foreground of the photograph is a magnificent Jaguar XK SS (chassis 707, engine 2066-9)—one of just sixteen such cars built prior to a fire at the Jaguar plant. The XK SS was a derivative of the legendary Jaguar D-type that racked up three consecutive wins at the 24 Hours of Le Mans. The XK SS carried a full windshield and bumperettes to make it roadworthy. Jaguar initially planned to build fifty of these appealing cars to meet the requirements for production car status in racing, but the factory fire destroyed parts and tooling, making this impossible. The sticker on this car's windshield is that of the Racing Drivers Club, founded in 1957.

This white Jaguar was initially imported for a driver who died in a racing accident before taking delivery. The first registered owners of the car were Sid and Alice Colberg of San Francisco, who acquired it in April 1958, trading in an older Aston Martin plus cash. Sid drove up to Sacramento and took delivery of the car from dealer Sam Weiss, whose wife Bobbie had her eyes on the Aston Martin. The Colbergs kept the XK SS for fourteen years before selling it for a handsome profit.

A Jaguar 3.8 sedan and an XK150 drophead rest behind the XK SS in the photograph, and a tall blond model in a gray ankle-length dress and long black gloves poses between the two cars.

On the program cover, a horizontal red band beneath the photograph carries text in black and yellow.

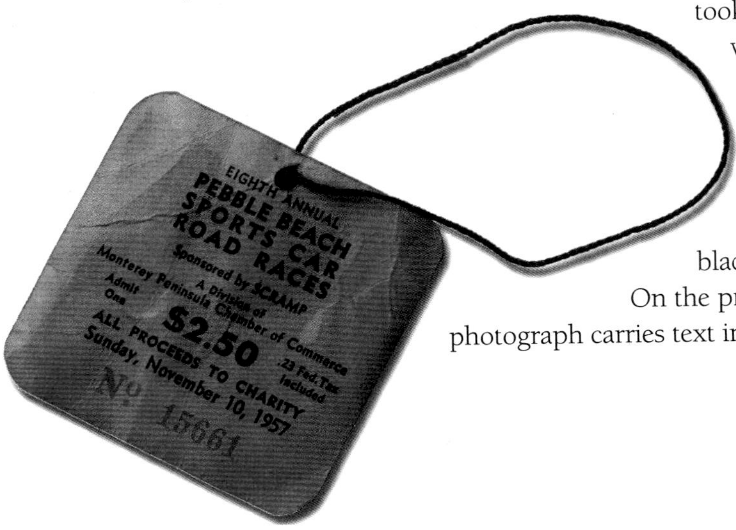

EIGHTH ANNUAL
PEBBLE BEACH
SPORTS CAR
ROAD RACES
Sponsored by SCRAMP
A Division of
Monterey Peninsula Chamber of Commerce
Admit One
$2.50
.23 Fed. Tax Included
ALL PROCEEDS TO CHARITY
Sunday, November 10, 1957
Nº 15661

8th Annual
NOVEMBER 9-10, 1957
PEBBLE BEACH AT LAGUNA SECA NATIONAL CHAMPIONSHIP
Sports Car ROAD RACES

1958 Julian P. Graham

Graphic art by Colden Whitman

■ THE FIRST POSTER CREATED SPECIFICALLY TO ADVERTISE THE PEBBLE BEACH CONCOURS D'ELEGANCE ROLLED OFF the presses in 1958. At the time, the Concours was still strongly linked with the Races in the minds and hearts of many participants. But the future was clear: the Concours would have to survive on its own.

To ensure that it did, Concours organizers worked hard to improve it. Most obviously, they built an awards ramp to enable spectators to better see winning entrants—and to add a dash of class. More importantly, they formally began to use the word *classics* in reference to prewar cars, carefully distinguishing them from antique and vintage cars, as well as more modern models. Increasingly, such classics would be the event's prime focus. Moreover, the 1958 Best of Show trophy was awarded to a 1930 duPont Town Car that J. B. Nethercutt had meticulously restored. That restoration would set the standard for years to come.

Organizers also publicized the Concours, and they declined to charge a fee for attendance.

The first Concours poster has a simple design, quite similar to posters created for the Road Race back in 1951 and 1952. It features a black-and-white photograph, taken by Pebble Beach's official photographer, Julian P. Graham, and bright yellow text, placed carefully by local graphic artist Colden Whitman.

The photograph actually dates back to 1953, but it is a beautiful overview of the Concours, shot from the elevated full-length balcony of Del Monte Lodge. That balcony, with Carmel Bay as backdrop, was among Graham's favorite locations; it afforded him the opportunity to take a variety of vertical and horizontal shots from many different angles. When taking the photograph used on the 1958 poster, Graham carefully lined up two tree trunks near the eighteenth green so they appear to be one.

The photograph shows Concours cars lined up by class in angular rows set off by chalk lines. A number of Jaguars in the foreground have hoods raised, apparently ready for judging. Spectators are plentiful, but they do not really constitute a crowd. The umbrellas toward the bottom of the photograph shade tables that are placed where Club XIX is now located.

Note the presence of golfers on the eighteenth green. At the Concours today, golfers are not in evidence. Knowing the damage that might be done by even one wayward slice, organizers now make certain that the eighteenth fairway is closed on Concours Sunday.

The original 1958 poster measures 11 by 13½ inches, and is printed on medium-weight cardboard stock.

9th Annual
PEBBLE BEACH
Concours D'Elegance
SATURDAY
NOVEMBER 8, 1958
11:00 A.M. - 5:00 P.M.
DEL MONTE LODGE
Pebble Beach, California
No Charge

1959 & 61 Julian P. Graham

Graphic art by Colden Whitman

■ THE PHOTOGRAPH ON THE 1959 PEBBLE BEACH CONCOURS D'ELEGANCE POSTER DID DOUBLE DUTY—AND MORE. As in other years, it also appeared on the cover of the program. And in 1961, the same photo was used again.

Something was amiss. Creativity was ebbing low.

Newspapers of the day reported that the Concours was known "throughout the country" as "the finest exhibition of museum-piece automobiles ever assembled." But, in truth, the event was still struggling to stand on its own.

In 1960, the Concours just didn't happen. Foul weather was said to be the reason. The event returned in 1961, but it lacked a certain amount of preparation and panache. No 1961 poster has been found, and it is uncertain if one was created. The program simply repeated the art and design of the 1959 program—though the date was changed and pink paper was used.

The photograph on the 1959 poster and the 1959 and 1961 program covers was taken at the 1958 Concours by Julian P. Graham, the official photographer at Pebble Beach. It captures the moment that announcer Jimmy Griffin and Mrs. Barry Wagner presented Dr. Milton R. Roth's 1934 Alfa Romeo Mille Miglia with its class ribbon. The car not only won the Prewar European Cars Class, it was eventually named the year's overall Reserve Winner—an award second only to Best of Show in the early years of the Concours.

On the poster the car is cropped short on both ends and on the bottom—often something to be avoided. But on this occasion, the cropping serves a purpose; it keeps the focal point on the action.

The photograph's strong vertical format also highlights some of Graham's favorite background scenery. To the left, two Monterey pine trees help frame the waters of Carmel Bay and Stillwater Cove, and Arch Rock, just ahead, helps to delineate those waters. The coastal headlands that lead to Carmel Valley can be seen in the distance. Golfers or spectators appear to be on the eighteenth green.

An elevated awards ramp was first used at the 1958 Concours, and just a hint of the ramp's safety posts and connecting lines can be seen at the very bottom left side of the image on the 1959 poster. On the program covers, more of the ramp is visible.

On the poster, graphic artist Colden Whitman placed the majority of text—all red on this occasion—in the upper right-hand corner, emerging from sea and sky.

The original 1959 poster measures 11 by 13½ inches, and is printed on medium-weight cardboard stock.

10th Annual
PEBBLE BEACH
Concours d'Elegance
SATURDAY
OCTOBER 24, 1959
11:00 A.M. - 5:00 P.M.
DEL MONTE LODGE
Pebble Beach, California
NO CHARGE

1962 Julian P. Graham

Graphic art by Colden Whitman

■ In the 1960s the Pebble Beach Concours d'Elegance dared to do what it hadn't done before: it asked entrants and spectators for a donation of one dollar. That donation enabled the Concours to benefit a local charitable endeavor.

Throughout the 1960s the Concours would benefit the local Community Hospital Auxiliary. Thereafter, it would benefit many other worthy causes—perhaps most notably the Pebble Beach Company Foundation and the United Way of Monterey County. These organizations, in turn, would help to publicize the Concours.

The 1962 Concours program cover made note of both the requested donation and the new beneficiary. It seems likely that a poster also would have been created to publicize these changes, but a 1962 poster has not been located.

In design, the 1962 program cover parallels preceding covers and posters, but it features a new photograph and has more visible reversed white text.

The photograph, taken by Pebble Beach official photographer Julian P. Graham, is an overview of a preceding Concours taken from the elevated location on The Lodge balcony that Graham often favored. The date is uncertain.

This particular overview is framed with foreground shrubbery and an overhead canopy of pine trees. A concession stand, with peaked awning and striped sides, is clearly visible to the left. In the background, golfers or spectators are visible on the eighteenth fairway of Pebble Beach Golf Links.

Graham has used a daylight filter, increasing contrast and reducing refracted light, in order to show the gentle wave action on the shore.

On the program cover, Colden Whitman has placed bright white text over the photograph in two places—at the top, in the canopy of pine branches, and at the bottom right, on the unoccupied lawn.

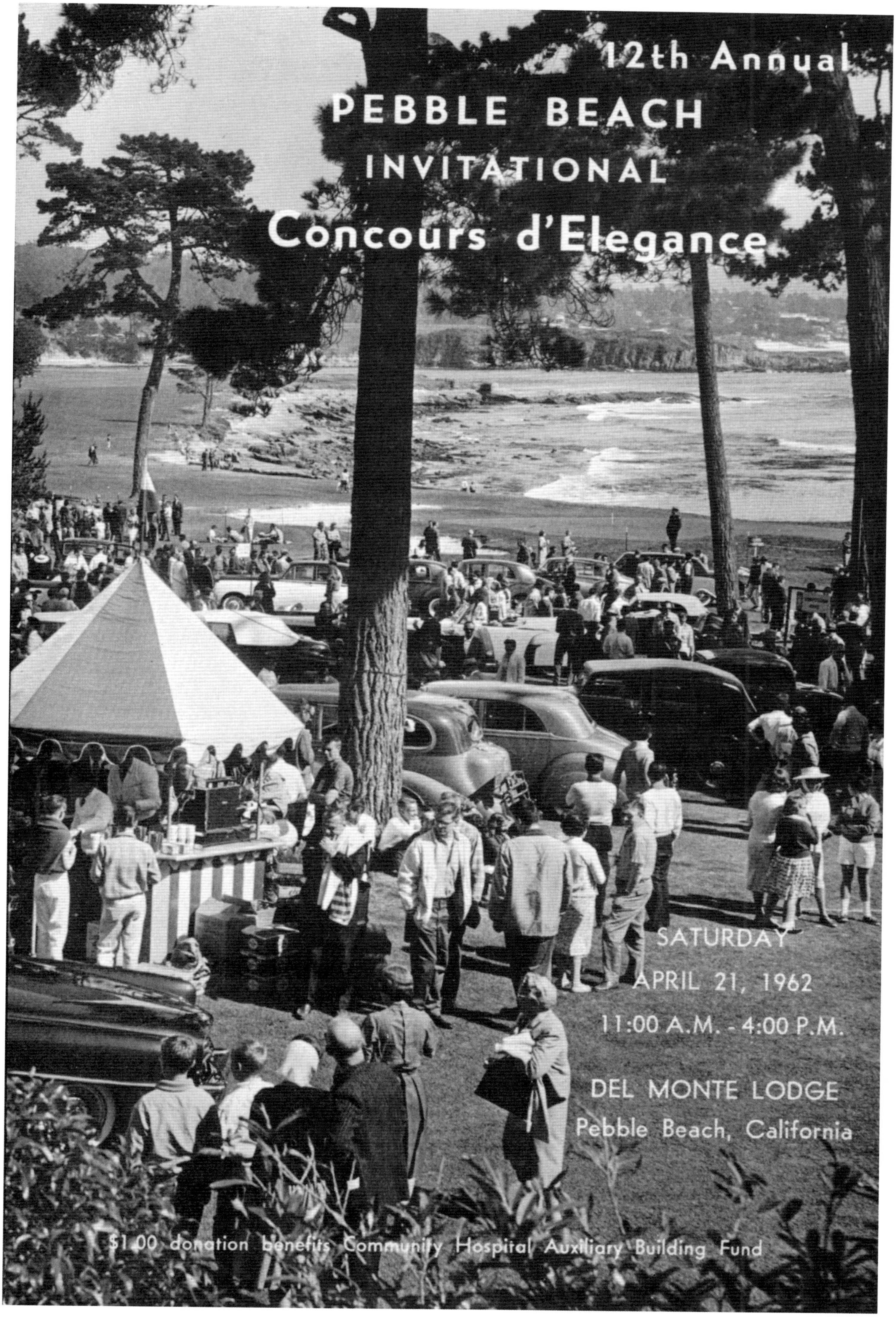

12th Annual

PEBBLE BEACH

INVITATIONAL

Concours d'Elegance

SATURDAY

APRIL 21, 1962

11:00 A.M. - 4:00 P.M.

DEL MONTE LODGE

Pebble Beach, California

$1.00 donation benefits Community Hospital Auxiliary Building Fund

1963 Julian P. Graham

Graphic art by Colden Whitman

■ WITH THE ADDITION OF ONE HORIZONTAL COLOR BAR AT ITS BASE TO HOLD THE MAJORITY OF TEXT, THE 1963 Pebble Beach Concours d'Elegance poster gained a fresh new look. This simple, but effective, redesign was the work of graphic artist Colden Whitman. To make certain the 1963 poster would capture the eye of passersby, Whitman chose to make this new color bar, and one line of upper text, bright red.

A photograph remains the focus of the poster, and that photograph is new, but its subject is not. Once again, the image features an overview of the Concours, taken by Pebble Beach official photographer Julian P. Graham from the elevated balcony of The Lodge. This photo also shows the entire eighteenth fairway of Pebble Beach Golf Links.

Graham has included many Monterey pines in this image, and judging by their small shadows the photograph was taken at about noon. Good contrast is evident: the soft light of the sky provides a dramatic backdrop to silhouette the pines.

The foreground in the photograph includes a hint of the awards ramp that was instituted back in 1958. A tall sign also designates the location of Class P for Rolls-Royce prewar closed cars; the wording and design of this sign effectively date the photograph to 1962.

Concours cars have been parked back-to-back at 90-degree angles in an attractive herringbone pattern. Their total number appears rather scant, but in fact a record number of approximately 130 cars took to the field that year. Entries had climbed steadily from the two to three dozen cars shown back in 1950. Today, however, the Concours hosts approximately 250 cars each year.

Unfortunately spectators at the 1963 Concours had to endure weather and scenery of a far different sort than depicted on this poster for the event. Continuous rain forced the 1963 Concours to move from the fragile Lodge lawn to a location near the start/finish line of the old racecourse.

The original 1963 poster measures 11 by 13½ inches and is printed on medium-weight cardboard stock.

13TH ANNUAL
PEBBLE BEACH
CONCOURS D'ELEGANCE

SATURDAY, APRIL 13, 1963 • 10 A.M. TO 4 P.M. • DEL MONTE LODGE, PEBBLE BEACH, CALIF.
$1.00 DONATION BENEFIT MONTEREY PENINSULA HOSPITAL AUXILIARY

1964 Julian P. Graham

Graphic art by Colden Whitman

■ BUT FOR A SLIGHT CHANGE IN COLOR, THE 1964 PEBBLE BEACH CONCOURS D'ELEGANCE POSTER DUPLICATES the design of the previous poster. Moreover, it features a near-duplicate photograph.

The photograph on the 1964 poster is again an overview taken by Pebble Beach official photographer Julian P. Graham from the elevated balcony of The Lodge. When compared to the photograph on the 1963 poster, it includes more of the awards ramp in the foreground and more of Carmel Bay to the right.

The placement and actions of spectators and entrants differ from picture to picture, but the cars remain the same. In this particular photograph, one entrant appears to be opening or closing the hood on his prewar Rolls-Royce Shooting Brake, otherwise known as a Woody Station Wagon.

The photographs on the 1963 and 1964 posters were probably snapped within minutes of each other in 1962.

Text on the poster is arranged almost exactly as the previous year, with the majority of text grouped in a horizontal bar of color at the bottom of the poster. But for 1964, graphic artist Colden Whitman has replaced the previous red of the top text and the bottom text box with a still brighter magenta.

The original 1964 poster measures 11 by 13½ inches and is printed on medium-weight cardboard stock.

14TH ANNUAL
PEBBLE BEACH
CONCOURS D'ELEGANCE
SATURDAY, MAY 9, 1964 • 10 A.M. TO 4 P.M. • DEL MONTE LODGE, PEBBLE BEACH, CALIF.
$1.00 DONATION BENEFIT COMMUNITY HOSPITAL AUXILIARY

1965 Colden Whitman

Photography by Julian P. Graham William C. Brooks

■ THE 1965 PEBBLE BEACH CONCOURS D'ELEGANCE DREW A RECORD NUMBER OF ENTRANTS. REGRETTABLY, THE event encountered bad weather and it had to be relocated yet again to the finishing straightaway of the old racecourse.

Several new design elements grace the 1965 Pebble Beach Concours d'Elegance poster, designed by local graphic artist Colden Whitman.

A photograph is still featured on the poster, but on this occasion, it is tinted a very light salmon pink, and it has a shouldered top, making room for added scrollwork at the poster's upper right and left corners. Most noticeably, just beneath the photograph, the poster utilizes bold new hand lettering to present the name of the event. This lettering gradually changes its size, shape, and color; the characters are first white, then black, then very vivid fuchsia. Additional text is presented in plain, black type at the very bottom of the poster, but it is framed by fuchsia-colored scrollwork.

The featured photograph, taken by Julian P. Graham or William C. Brooks, focuses on a brass era car crossing the display ramp during a previous Concours. The car is a right-hand-drive open touring vehicle, with spoke wheels and hard rubber tires, and without provision for a top of any sort. Accompanying the car and its driver across the ramp are three young boys who seem enthralled with the crowd that surrounds them.

The image emphasizes the foreground. In the background, pine trees frame the expansive scenery of Stillwater Cove and the eighteenth fairway of Pebble Beach Golf Links.

The original poster measures 11 by 13½ inches and is printed on medium-weight cardboard stock.

15TH annual PEBBLE BEACH CONCOURS D'ELEGANCE

SATURDAY, APRIL 17, 1965 • 11 A.M. - 4 P.M. • DEL MONTE LODGE • PEBBLE BEACH CALIFORNIA • DONATION $1.00 • BENEFIT COMMUNITY HOSPITAL AUXILIARY

1966 Eldon Dedini

■ 1966 MARKED THE BEGINNING OF A NEW ERA IN POSTER DESIGN FOR THE PEBBLE BEACH CONCOURS D'ELEGANCE.

Previous posters had consistently paired photographs with text—a common poster style throughout much of the 1940s and 1950s. And all of the more recent Concours posters had specifically featured black-and-white overviews of the event. Though elegant, they no longer drew the eye. One poster might easily be the next.

Elsewhere, a new age was dawning; the art world in general—and poster art in particular—was in transition. In New York, Andy Warhol was enjoying more than fifteen minutes of fame. And just up the coast in San Francisco, the psychedelic rock poster had recently been born.

The Pebble Beach Concours needed to liven up its look. And it was cartoonist Eldon Dedini who helped it do that.

Born in King City, California, in 1921, Eldon Dedini was almost immediately obsessed with drawing all that he saw. At age five, he could fill a nickel sketchpad with one morning's efforts. To save nickels, a chalkboard was soon hung on the kitchen wall.

After high school, Dedini first attended Salinas Junior College, now Hartnell College, and then the Chouinard Art Institute in Los Angeles. Upon graduation, he initially drew storyboards for Universal Studios, and then he went to work for the Walt Disney Company. In his spare time, he drew cartoons for *Esquire* magazine. When *Esquire* asked him to accept a full-time position, he readily agreed, knowing that he could live wherever he desired and work from home. He moved to Carmel in 1950 to be near family. His cartoons have also appeared in *The New Yorker* and *Playboy* magazines, and he is a member of the National Cartoonists Society.

Dedini had previously designed just one poster—to publicize a charity concert by Joan Baez—when he was first approached to do the 1966 poster for the Concours. It was Rody Holt, a volunteer with the Community Hospital Auxiliary, then the Concours' benefiting charity, who did the asking; she had seen the Baez poster and was impressed by it. Dedini quickly agreed to her request, and set to work.

He initially did two rough sketches in very different styles—and he was prepared to do more if need be. When Holt and Concours organizers Gwenn Graham and Carol Rissel saw the roughs, they liked both and couldn't decide between them. John B. Morse, former President of Del Monte Properties Company, settled the matter, saying, "Let's do both of them."

Dedini's first 1966 poster was done in the tradition of German Jugendstil artists, whose late nineteenth century prints featured hand lettering and designs that often looked like woodcuts.

Dedini's choice of style matches his subject—a turn-of-the-century couple in period clothing befitting a tour in an open-air horseless carriage. The two people are sitting upright—he sports a broad white moustache but she is probably better protected from the elements, with goggles, scarf, and plumed hat! The carriage, shown in caramel and black, is an amalgam of designs of the era. Details include sizable headlights and scuttle-mounted sidelights, a running board, a folded top, and winged fenders.

A bold red background provides a necessarily strong contrast for the predominantly black subject and the black text at the top and bottom of the poster. White is used to accent two elements: the couple's face and the event's date.

Dedini's signature is in the bottom right corner.

The original artwork for this 1966 poster, which is a rough, measures 24 by 36 inches. It went to press without much refinement in order to retain its starkness.

continued

CONCOURS 16th ANNUAL

d'ÉLEGANCE

SAT. JULY 23rd

BENEFIT COMMUNITY HOSPITAL AUXILIARY

DEL MONTE LODGE

PEBBLE BEACH California

1966 Eldon Dedini continued

THE SECOND POSTER CREATED BY ELDON DEDINI FOR THE 1966 CONCOURS DRAWS UPON THE WORK OF FAMED French poster artist Henri de Toulouse-Lautrec. In fact, it parallels Lautrec's first poster, "Moulin Rouge—La Goulue," to an amazing degree.

"I've always loved Toulouse-Lautrec," says Dedini. "That's why I've stolen as much as I could from him!"

Dedini has placed an English Rolls-Royce at center stage, where La Goulue danced the cancan on the original poster. The Rolls-Royce, in mustard with black-and-white accents, includes Flying Lady mascot, massive headlights, and whitewall tires. It is angled to show such details as fender line, long hood with side louvers, rear-hinged door, landau bar on top, and the outline of a trunk.

In Dedini's work, La Goulue and Jane Avril (note the ladies with red hair) and other recognizable characters from Lautrec's café scenes appear in the crowd. Dedini refers to the man at the car's left rear bumper as the "Duke of Del Monte." The black silhouettes of several other spectators can also be seen.

In the foreground, Dedini offers his impression of Toulouse-Lautrec—the bearded man with dark glasses, hat, and cane.

The typography and the color scheme of Dedini's poster are also modeled closely on the original.

"I don't know how many people followed all of this when they saw the poster," says Dedini. "But I think it makes an exciting scene. And that's exactly what a poster should be."

Dedini wanted his poster to entice people to see the Concours. He was neither a photographer, nor an industrial designer. He was a cartoonist, trying to create a fantasy that would draw people in.

Dedini's signature appears beside Toulouse-Lautrec's cane.

The original artwork for this 1966 poster measures 18 by 24 inches.

When it was time to go to press, Concours organizers decided to not only print both posters, they decided to print each of them in multiple sizes. They reasoned that this would increase the number of possible store placements. If a full-size poster was too large for a particular store window, a smaller version would be available—as would handbills and even postcards. The latter could easily be displayed near cash registers.

Ultimately, the posters were a hit. The original artwork was offered as a gate prize at the Concours. Extra printed posters that had not been placed in store windows were later sold at the Community Hospital for $2 and $5, depending on size. One savvy Carmel gallery owner bought the posters in bulk, and resold them at a substantial profit.

With Dedini as their creator, Concours posters were evolving from publicity piece to collectible.

CONCOURS d'ELEGANCE
DEL MONTE LODGE • PEBBLE BEACH, CAL.
SATURDAY JULY 23 1966
16th annual
Benefit
Community
Hospital
Auxiliary

1967 Eldon Dedini

■ The Pebble Beach Concours d'Elegance had long drawn its fair share of noted personalities, but in 1967, Bob Hope suddenly stepped up to the mike and wowed the crowd. The local *Game & Gossip* magazine later reported on Hope's presence, saying he was truly the "star" on the show field that day. But it also noted in the very next sentence that poster artist Eldon Dedini had played "the best supporting role" in the show. Concours organizers and participants all recognized the contribution that Dedini was making.

The 1967 Concours poster, which features a detail of a car window with the face of a single female passenger, underscores cartoonist Eldon Dedini's understanding of the atmosphere of the Pebble Beach Concours d'Elegance. It is all about style.

This poster carries a series of ovals to perfection. The oval of the window is most obvious, of course, but the oval shape is repeated on the carriage's side lamp, in the roundness of the woman's face, and in the background shading.

The illustration was first done in black and white, and that simple uncolored image was reproduced on early posters, on program covers, on tickets, and other items. Dedini then did six or seven roughs showing possible color schemes for the final poster image. Those color roughs were eventually framed and sold in what might well have been the Concours' first poster art auction.

The colors on the final 1967 poster are arresting. The carriage is basic black, but its landau bar and side lamp are mustard yellow. Red frames the primary image and is also used as an accent—in the plumes on a hat and the flame of the lamp. The midnight blue background color spills through the window, intermingling with the woman's brocade dress and providing subtle shadows.

The artist has done his own graphics, hand-lettering all key text, which is grouped in the bottom third of the poster. The only text that is typeset is the mention that the Concours is a benefit.

Dedini's signature is on the right, near the base of the primary image.

The original 1967 color poster measures 18 by 24 inches and is a serigraph, an original silk-screen print with each color printed separately.

Concours d'Elegance
DEL MONTE LODGE · PEBBLE BEACH
17th ANNUAL
BENEFIT COMMUNITY HOSPITAL AUXILIARY
AUGUST 12

1968 Eldon Dedini

■ As in 1966, Eldon Dedini roughed out two possible posters for the 1968 Pebble Beach Concours d'Elegance. But heading in to his meeting with Concours organizers, he left one of the posters in his car. "It was just *too* rough," he says.

The meeting proceeded, the poster was approved, and plans were made for its printing and distribution. At the last minute, before leaving, Dedini ran out to his car, grabbed the rough, and gave the organizers just a glimpse of it.

They loved it.

Ultimately, it was that rough that became the primary poster for the eighteenth annual Concours.

The image on the primary 1968 poster was inspired by a 1902 Sears horseless carriage owned by Pebble Beach resident Alton Walker, who served as Chairman of the very first Pebble Beach Concours. Dedini had visited Walker's garage and was awed by what he saw. In illustrating the turn-of-the-century vehicle, Dedini emphasizes a few key details—its large wheels, its almost vertical steering column, its side lamps, and its folded top. Note the complete lack of a windshield.

Seated in the carriage is a woman in a high-collared black dress. Her only protection from the elements is her wide sun hat with plumes. A man in the foreground, likely the car's driver, is somewhat more defined. His facial features are enlarged, and he sports long sideburns. A modish man, he wears an olive green suit with magenta pinstripes that emphasize the tapered legs and tail. A vest with a hint of pattern bunches up above the man's slight potbelly, and accessories include blue tie, hat, and cufflinks. Hands in pockets, he is quite the natty fellow.

Unfinished areas of the image add to, rather than detract from, the overall design—an indication of quality work by an artist who understands essence.

The text appears at the top left and at the bottom of the poster, and Dedini's signature appears in the lower right corner.

The original artwork for this 1966 poster is 24 by 36 inches. It was printed as a serigraph.

continued

18th annual
Concours d' Elegance
June 2nd
Del Monte Lodge
Pebble Beach Cal.
BENEFIT COMMUNITY HOSPITAL AUXILIARY

1968 Eldon Dedini continued

The poster that Eldon Dedini originally presented to Concours organizers in 1968 was eventually used on smaller posters, the program cover, various bulletins, and tickets.

This particular artwork features "a fanciful Rolls-Royce," per Dedini. The automobile's front end is treated with a mushroom effect; enlarged front fender wings flare out over the tires, and the use of bright magenta highlights their bulbous curves. Headlights and road lamps, located just above the car's twin-blade bumper, are also enlarged. The marque's classic radiator shell and Flying Lady ornament appear at front and center, and a very long and narrow hood sweeps back to the windshield.

"That car's a fantastic shape," said Dedini when reviewing the poster again recently. He admits that all the cars on his Concours posters were rather "free-form." As a cartoonist, Dedini generally avoided pure illustration, seeking instead to offer his personal interpretation of cars.

This car's passengers are caricatured as well. Grouped tightly in the car are five exaggerated individuals in late 1920s dress. A Toulouse-Lautrec–type character is positioned in the center.

On the whole, this image is more refined in style than the image used on the primary 1968 poster. The two designs might have clashed, but Dedini resolved the potential conflict by utilizing the same bright magenta on both posters. The same hand lettering is also used.

"My lettering was kind of wild," Dedini says. "But it works, I think. Enough time goes by, and even I like it!"

Dedini's signature appears in the lower right corner.

The original artwork for this 1968 poster is 18 by 24 inches. It was printed as a serigraph.

18th annual
Concours d'Elegance
BENEFIT COMMUNITY HOSPITAL AUXILIARY
DEL MONTE
LODGE
PEBBLE
BEACH
JUNE
2

1969 Eldon Dedini

■ THROUGH MUCH OF ITS EARLY HISTORY, THE PEBBLE BEACH Concours d'Elegance was under the guidance of Gwenn Graham, who handled publicity for Del Monte Properties Company and was married to photographer Julian P. Graham. Gwenn Graham died in 1968, and for three years thereafter, the Concours and its Best of Show Trophy were renamed in her honor.

The poster for the 1969 Gwenn Graham Concours was the fourth consecutive poster created by cartoonist Eldon Dedini. It was also the Concours' first horizontal poster.

The featured automobile, depicted in side profile running across the poster's mid-section, began life as a Rolls-Royce, but quickly morphed into a Duesenberg-like phaeton. Its pre-1933 body, with nonskirted fenders and side-mounted spare tires carried high above the descending fender line, is a deep French blue, and Dedini has embellished the body with numerous styling cues. Red is applied to the underside of fenders and the interior upholstery. And a deep mustard color is applied liberally elsewhere.

Four black-and-white cartoon characters in the car bring the poster to life. The couple in front is juxtaposed with the couple in the back, and both the male driver and lady in the rear compartment have swung a leg out over the running board, posing provocatively for viewers. Their clothing dates to the late 1920s or early 1930s. "I kind of like those crazy people," says Dedini. "They're *Great Gatsby* / F. Scott Fitzgerald types. Think Robert Redford and his crew." Of course, the poster predates the 1974 movie.

With car and characters completed, Dedini struggled to find the right background. He tried foliage, he tried pine trees, he tried half a dozen other possibilities, debating them one by one with his wife, Virginia, a graphic artist. With the time for debate at an end and the printer's deadline looming, he finally settled on a multicolored sky that is part Vincent van Gogh, part rock poster.

"It was the era of the psychedelic, the experimental," says Dedini. "Nothing was traditional. And the lettering and the dots were definitely influenced by the times."

The graphic text appears at the bottom of the poster and repeats the green, orange, and red of the sky. Dedini has signed the poster in the bottom right corner.

This poster was one of Dedini's favorite works, and the original artwork remains in his possession. The artwork—a collage—measures 36 by 24 inches.

The original 1969 poster, printed in multiple sizes, is a serigraph.

th ANNUAL
DEL MONTE LODGE PEBBLE BEACH
BENEFIT COMMUNITY
HOSPITAL AUXILIARY
1969
CONCOURS
MAY 31

1970 Eldon Dedini

■ For his fifth consecutive Concours poster, in 1970, cartoonist Eldon Dedini drew inspiration from two distinctly different sources—the bicentennial of Monterey and the flourishing counterculture movement of the day.

It was back in 1770 that Franciscan Father Junipero Serra first established the Mission and Presidio of San Carlos de Borromeo de Monterey in order to minister to local tribes. That Mission, which moved to Carmel the next year, appears in the background of Dedini's 1970 poster, toward the top right corner. Blue skies, sand, board fences, and just a hint of cypress trees put the Mission in context.

The foreground of the poster features a brass era touring car, in black, with brass accents on the radiator, the lights, the outside hand brake, and the gear shift controls.

The car is packed full of passengers—monks and Native Americans, in this case—all ready to go for a ride. Another monk prepares to crank up the motor. They are oblivious to any damage the sand might cause to their touring car. Everyone has the same happy "What, me worried?" look on their faces. Their attitude, in line with that of the then-flourishing hippie counterculture, is "Let's all just get along." It's clear from the word *amor* on the side of the car and the daisies in their hands that the passengers believe in peace, love, and flower power.

The illustration is bounded on three sides by a black border, which is broken just briefly at the top with mention of the Concours' benefiting charity. The majority of text runs along the bottom of the poster, in clear red type on white.

Dedini has signed the poster on the lower right side.

The original artwork for the 1970 poster measures 36 by 24 inches. The poster, printed in multiple sizes, is a serigraph.

BENEFIT COMMUNITY HOSPITAL AUXILIARY
URS DEL MONTE LODGE PEBBLE BEACH MAY 30 1970

1971 Eldon Dedini

■ Each time he was asked to design a Concours poster, cartoonist Eldon Dedini went in search of something new. "I wanted to find something that interested me," he says. "I didn't want to use a cliché or redo the previous year's poster."

In his sixth consecutive year as poster artist, new ideas were getting a bit more difficult to come by. Ultimately, he found what he needed in an old catalog for an 1892 Panhard. It was a picture of people—not the car—that initially caught his eye.

"As a cartoonist, I always started with the people, and the car came along later," he confesses. "I knew the car was the point, and I was not going to downgrade it. But the Concours is a people event; it's for people who love cars."

Dedini had spotted a family photograph of the carmaker René Panhard, his wife, and his two young daughters out for a Sunday drive. The photograph captured the essence of concours events in their infancy—in France at the turn of the nineteenth century.

Dedini recalls the moment that inspiration hit: "I saw the photo and I thought, 'That's charming.' Then I read the caption, and I said, 'There's my poster!' I knew it immediately. And so I simply drew the scene, in my way, and I wrote the photo caption right beside it."

On the poster, Dedini's drawing appears without the fanfare of embellishment or the addition of color. Yet the black-and-white, fairly true-to-life translation of that historic photograph immediately captures the eye and the imagination.

The poster does make use of bright color in other areas. Thick red and mustard stripes alternate across the top of the poster, and the same colors are repeated in the text block that runs across the bottom.

Dedini's signature is located in the bottom right corner of the black-and-white drawing.

The original artwork for the 1971 poster measures 24 by 36 inches. The poster, printed in multiple sizes, is a serigraph.

René Panhard
with his wife and
children go for
a Sunday drive
in an 1892 Panhard
21th ANNUAL
GWENN GRAHAM CONCOURS · MAY 29 1971
DEL MONTE LODGE · PEBBLE BEACH
BENEFIT
COMMUNITY
HOSPITAL
AUXILIARY

1972 Eldon Dedini

■ THROUGH MUCH OF THE LATE 1960S AND EARLY 1970S, PARTICULARLY AFTER THE DEATH OF ORGANIZER Gwenn Graham, the reputation of the Pebble Beach Concours d'Elegance was in decline; entries were less than stellar, judgments seemed questionable, and spectators were few in number. But in 1972, two men reversed that trend. Lorin Tryon and Jules "J." Heumann took the Concours in hand and immediately changed many things: a radical new judging process was implemented, class categories were revised, and only the most spectacular cars were invited to attend.

The response was overwhelmingly positive. And in ensuing years, under the ongoing guidance of J. and Lorin, the Concours would develop into a world class event.

While other things changed in 1972, the poster artist remained the same; cartoonist Eldon Dedini created his seventh consecutive poster for the Pebble Beach Concours. This poster relies entirely on the use of just two colors—a rich purple and black—against a white background that is often brought to the fore in illustrations.

Intricate graphics, scrollwork, and double line surrounds divide the poster into three distinct horizontal panels, each comprising both text and illustration. The eye is drawn first to the center panel, which dominates the other two in size. Here, Dedini has placed a caricature of an older man accompanied by a younger woman. The two are clothed in their finest attire for the Concours, and the man graciously tips his hat to a passerby—or to the viewer. Dedini says the work of Jacques Lartique, a turn-of-the-century French photographer, influenced some of the details, particularly the costumes and postures.

Automobiles appear in all three panels. The upper panel includes an Antique touring car, with dog in the backseat, ready to go. The lower panel includes a sporty Vintage two-seater with a rounded monocle windshield mounted to the steering column. The front of another Vintage car is just visible at left in the center panel. Dedini presents all of these vehicles in some detail while allowing the viewer to guess their marques.

The text is displayed in all three panels. The title of the event, the Pebble Beach Concours d'Elegance, is placed over the center image of the couple, and the date is also placed in the middle panel. The location of the event appears at the bottom of the poster, and additional information, including mention of a new charity, appears at the top. The new charity on this occasion is Guide Dogs for the Blind.

Dedini's signature appears in the lower right corner.

The original 1972 poster measures 24 by 36 inches and is a serigraph.

22nd Annual
BENEFIT
GUIDE DOGS
FOR THE BLIND
SUNDAY
AUG. 6
1972
AY201
PEBBLE BEACH
Concours d'Elegance
Del Monte Lodge
Dedini

1973 Eldon Dedini

■ ELDON DEDINI TOOK A STEP INTO PURE FANTASY WITH HIS 1973 POSTER FOR THE PEBBLE BEACH CONCOURS d'Elegance. He himself says it looks "a bit surreal."

When he first set to work in 1973, Dedini had one concern in mind: Color-Ad, his regular printer, was busy, and the printing job would be farmed out.

"I thought, I better make it simple, since I wouldn't be in control," he says.

Dedini started with a big color block that eventually became sky. A second color block signaled ground and a rising moon. As was generally his practice, Dedini choose all of these colors from the printer's color chart to ensure the fidelity of the reproduction.

The poster's two primary subjects appear in simple black and white. The first of these, a flying car, is transporting two occupants, a man and a woman, across a galaxy of stars. A long, flowing scarf trails behind both the woman and the car, projecting the freedom and joy of this alternate world. Dedini says he drew car after car "until I got one I liked."

Down on the ground, the second subject, a woman, is seen waving her handkerchief, bidding the couple adieu. Sadly, in 1973, Eldon Dedini, too, would bid adieu to the Concours—for a time. After creating eight consecutive Concours posters, he felt it was time to move on. But he would return again to design the poster for the Concours' fortieth anniversary.

All of the text on the 1973 poster runs across the bottom, beneath the illustration. And on this occasion, the text is set in type.

Dedini's signature appears just beneath the bottom right corner of his illustration.

The original 1973 poster measures 24 by 36 inches and is a serigraph.

Dedini
23 RD ANNUAL PEBBLE BEACH CONCOURS d'ELEGANCE 1973
DEL MONTE LODGE - SUNDAY AUGUST 12 BENEFIT
GUIDE DOGS FOR
THE BLIND, INC

1974 Colden Whitman

Photography by Julian P. Graham William C. Brooks

■ In 1974, following the eight years of Eldon Dedini's whimsical and cartoon-like poster images, local graphic artist Colden Whitman returned to design what would be the last Pebble Beach Concours d'Elegance poster based on photography until the turn of the century.

This poster differs substantially from the multitude of photography-based posters that were previously used.

Filling slightly more than the lower half of the poster are photographs of five antique and vintage cars. A Packard, on the right side of the poster, and a Darracq, to the lower left, are the most readily identified. All of the car photographs, taken most likely by Julian P. Graham or William C. Brooks at past Concours, have been further divided into twelve boxed sections that provide graphic uniformity. And they have been printed in selected shades of orange, gold, maroon, and rust red. The rest of the poster also utilizes these colors.

Informational text is grouped together in the poster's upper left corner. Primary text appears in a nicely stylized sans serif font with deep drop shadows.

A cluster of multicolored balloons that are loosely tethered to the Packard helps to integrate the top and bottom portions of the poster.

Note that the Monterey Peninsula United Fund is mentioned and its logo appears amidst the cars. This charitable organization—now the United Way of Monterey County—first joined forces with the Pebble Beach Concours d'Elegance in 1974, and the two remain strongly linked today. The United Way is one of the primary recipients of charitable contributions from the Concours, and in return it often helps to gather needed volunteers, publicize the event, and oversee numerous other tasks. In 1974 the Fund provided the décor for the Concours; in keeping with the image on this poster, they anchored multicolored balloons to The Lodge balcony and to class signs on the field.

The year also saw another union—actually a reunion of sorts. With the blessing of officials at Pebble Beach, the first Monterey Historic Automobile Races were held at Laguna Seca on the Saturday preceding the Concours. The Concours was once again paired with car races, and that remains true to this day. The two events are held concurrently each year.

24 ANNUAL

PEBBLE BEACH CONCOURS d'ELEGANCE

SUN. AUG. 11, 74

AT DEL MONTE LODGE

1975 Dick Cole

■ THE PEBBLE BEACH CONCOURS D'ELEGANCE CELEBRATED ITS SILVER ANNIVERSARY IN 1975, AND ALL WAS WELL. Entries were of increasingly high quality. Judges—and their decisions—were respected. And attendance was rapidly rising.

To mark the occasion, Concours organizers commissioned artist Dick Cole to do a special illustration for that year's poster. Cole had a real affinity for automobiles. Born in Santa Cruz, Dick Cole grew up in Southern California as hot rods and drag racing came of age. He once professed that his high school years were spent "drawing cartoons of self-destructing V8 engines in Model A's."

Following a stint in the U.S. Air Force, he focused on his education, first earning a Bachelor of Fine Arts from the University of California at Los Angeles, then attending the Art Center School in Los Angeles, now Art Center College of Design in Pasadena, California. He eventually joined the Galli, Bomberger, Hansen and Dumas group in San Francisco, working on national marketing campaigns. Then, after a partnership with designer Primo Angeli, he started his own freelance business, eventually opening studios in both San Francisco and Palo Alto and working primarily with educational publishers. Cole is a past President of the San Francisco Society of Illustrators, and he has taught courses in illustration at Foothill College in Los Altos Hills and at the Academy of Art College, San Francisco.

Using a limited palette but making dramatic use of the white illustration board as a positive, Cole's 1975 poster features a front three-quarter profile of a left-hand-drive Springfield-built Rolls-Royce Phantom I Town Car. The majority of the chauffeur-driven car is in negative black, but silver sunlight accents numerous features. On the original poster a silver metallic ink is used. In the reproduction on page 57 these silver sections appear gray.

Depth of field is established by the receding lines on the vehicle and the forested area in the upper left. The first line of trees and foliage in the forest are painted with lighter shades and the color deepens to black as the eye is drawn into the forest, away from the light.

Two slightly wavy horizontal bars of silver run across the upper segment of the poster suggesting the ocean that might be in the distance. Black and silver textual graphics appear in the upper right corner and at the bottom of the poster.

On the whole, Dick Cole presents a classical yet subtle statement of elegance.

During the 1975 Concours, the original artwork for the poster was auctioned off by Merv Griffin to benefit the Monterey Peninsula United Fund.

PEBBLE BEACH
CONCOURS d' ELEGANCE

SUNDAY, AUGUST 10, 1975 AT DEL MONTE LODGE

1976 Ed Greco

■ IN ONE BOLD, EYE-CATCHING SCENE, THE 1976 CONCOURS POSTER CAPTURES THE COMPLETE PEBBLE BEACH experience. The artist, Ed Greco, has painted a Packard that depicts all the glamour of the classic era, and he has surrounded the car with different scenes from the Concours.

The car itself is placed boldly in the center of the poster. It faces almost directly forward, but its wheels are turned to reveal their sporty wire spokes and whitewall tires. The huge fenders appear exaggerated in front of the long hood line flowing from the narrow windshield. While the car has the shouldered radiator common to classic Packards, it appears to be an impressionistic composite rather than a literal presentation. Details include twin wind deflectors abutting the windshield and the single driver-side-mounted spare tire. A hint of undercarriage is seen between the left front brake drum and tire. The car gleams and sparkles with red and gold reflections.

To the right of the vehicle, three Concours judges, clipboards in hand, compare notes and opinions. They are an interesting threesome. The group includes a woman, though just two women had served as judges in the Concours' early years, and one man sports a bowler hat—just as illustrious Judge Lucius Beebe once did. To the left, three spectators enjoy the social atmosphere of the event. Finally, a photographer kneels close to the car to catch the essential close-up shot.

This interesting scene is superimposed over a solid dark red and white painting of a *Great Gatsby*-style man wearing a field cap and holding a thin cigarillo cigar between his fingers. He is staring moodily out of the poster, directly at the viewer, adding an air of intrigue and mystery to the image. The red of the background gives the poster boldness and visual impact and contrasts well with the gold and black of the car, while variety is added in the subtle tones of the clothing of the men and women.

The way the car and its background are depicted clearly reflects Greco's long career in advertising and his deep appreciation for the automobile. Savoring its appearance of power and stunning design, he emphasizes the best features of the car while leaving details to the imagination of the viewer.

Greco has spent all his life in California, living mostly on the Monterey Peninsula. As a child he was always sketching and drawing, and he began his poster design career in high school. He attended Santa Clara University, majoring in economics, and on graduation, he worked for a local newspaper group, designing advertising and honing his marketing skills. Over the years, he has been a freelance designer and he has run his own agency, specializing in banking and defense-related clients. He also has owned a variety of classic cars.

On his poster, Greco's signature appears near the front right tire of the car.

The original artwork for the 1976 poster, painted in acrylics on illustration board, measures 20 by 30 inches. It was donated to the Concours' charities.

TWENTY-SIXTH ANNUAL
CONCOURS d'ELEGANCE
Pebble Beach
SUNDAY, AUGUST 29, 1976 AT DEL MONTE LODGE

1977 Bill Hinds

■ WHEN FIRST APPROACHED BY PEBBLE BEACH CONCOURS ORGANIZERS TO CREATE THE poster art for their 1977 event, artist Bill Hinds drafted a number of sketches featuring various classic cars. But when he learned that Bugatti—his favorite marque—was to be featured that year, he immediately shifted focus.

His final poster features what appears to be a chance meeting of two Bugattis—the 1927 Type 37 Grand Prix (chassis number 37207) on the right and the 1936 Type 57 Drophead Coupé built by Graber on the left.

Coincidentally, Hinds had just returned from the U.S. Grand Prix in Long Beach, California, where a preliminary race was held for vintage cars. At this meet, René Dreyfus, ex-Bugatti team driver, was on hand to race the 1927 Bugatti Type 37. Prior to that race, Hinds, along with the car's owner, Carlton Coolidge, test drove the Bugatti on the Long Beach track. The sheer thrill of this experience, plus the imposing image of Dreyfus behind the wheel, were forefront in Hinds' mind as he composed his Concours poster. The other car in the picture—the Type 57—had long been owned by Charles deLimur and had recently undergone a complete restoration.

Coolidge, deLimur, and Hinds have all served as judges at the Pebble Beach Concours d'Elegance.

Bill Hinds' love of the automobile began at an early age. "During my high school years I was recognized as a car freak," recalls Hinds. He was just fifteen when he caught his first glimpse of a Bugatti—a Type 35 Grand Prix car—and it was love at first sight.

In his formative years Hinds drew his artistic inspiration from television, films, and books. Early French poster art caught his eye and his imagination. Hinds attributes much of his later artistic development to his relocation to the Monterey Peninsula. This mecca of creativity has long drawn artistic souls from near and far, and Hinds believes the Monterey area to be "the cradle of American bohemia, where prosperous artisans live in the pursuit of beauty and live life as art—body, mind and spirit."

It was in Monterey that he began the study of the French curve—a sweeping design feature perfected by the French, which accentuates the dramatic flair of the French automobile. Indeed, the body of the Bugatti Type 57 contains some of these famous curves.

Hinds completed three studies for the 1977 poster before he decided upon the artwork we see today—the surreal image of two Bugattis suspended in space. He chose primary colors, red and blue with a lesser splash of yellow, to produce a striking effect, with the rising sun casting long shadows and highlighting intricate details of the wheels, crank handle, and rear bumper. He painted most of the poster in his Monterey automotive restoration shop—and he often painted while astride a ladder, looking down at cars to gain the right perspective!

The original artwork for the 1977 poster is a mélange of materials, including enamel, gold leaf, and poster paint on tempered plywood measuring 18 by 25 inches. The artwork was sold at auction.

concours
d'elegance
Del Monte Lodge
28, 1977
11

11

1978 Dong Sun Kim

■ IN CREATING THE POSTER ART FOR THE 1978 PEBBLE BEACH CONCOURS, LOCAL ARTIST DONG SUN KIM HAS drawn an intimate scene in contrast to the flamboyance of other years.

Unusually, the rear view of a chauffeur-driven antique touring car is featured. The top is in place, but without side curtains, and judging from the strength of the shadows, it is a very sunny day. A stylish couple is shown exiting the rear door; the gentleman, clad in a duster and sporting a field cap, takes the hand of his bonneted lady as she steps down from the running board to the ground.

Kim's artwork is highly stylized. Long shadows accent the gentleman and his motorcar. The car's wooden spoke wheels are particularly visible in the undercarriage shadow. The color palette contains shades of neutral brown, tan, and light cream that complement the more abstract wooded background.

An array of colorful balloons is magically set aloft at the time of the lady's arrival. In their merry flight into a blue and lightly clouded sky, the balloons are like the bubbles in champagne.

The scene is one of pure fantasy—a reminder of a more innocent and peaceful time.

That there is less emphasis in this poster on the style and design of the car might be a reflection of the artist's background. Kim is a native of Seoul, South Korea, and he was educated and worked there for many years. His education did not include any formal art training although he worked his way through the University of Seoul, graduating with honors, by painting large architectural murals. Afterward, he joined the Korean Marines, serving for sixteen years as an intelligence officer.

In December 1977, Kim followed his older brother to the United States, settling on the Monterey Peninsula and hoping to support his family as an artist. He found work in a restaurant in Moss Landing, and it was there that his career as a painter of murals began when he persuaded the restaurant's owner to allow him to paint a blank interior wall. Since then he has painted murals in many other local buildings, including the Pacheco Club in Monterey, Flaherty's Oyster Bar & Seafood Grill, and Bruno's Market & Deli in Carmel. His work can still be seen in all of these locations.

Kim's mural work has since changed into something very eye-catching in contrast to today's world of standard Madison Avenue–generated advertising billboards and logos. As one travels through the rich agricultural basket of Salinas, California, one can see in the fields alongside Interstate 101 and Highway 68, massive eighteen-foot-high cutouts of farmworkers harvesting and packing lettuce. Kim has worked with other artists to create these unique and often highly personalized pieces that sometimes also include ranch owners and family members.

The artist's signature on the 1978 poster can be found in the shadow at the rear of the car. The original artwork for the poster, done with oils on canvas and completed in sixteen hours, measures 24 by 36 inches. Kim donated the painting to the Concours to be sold for charity.

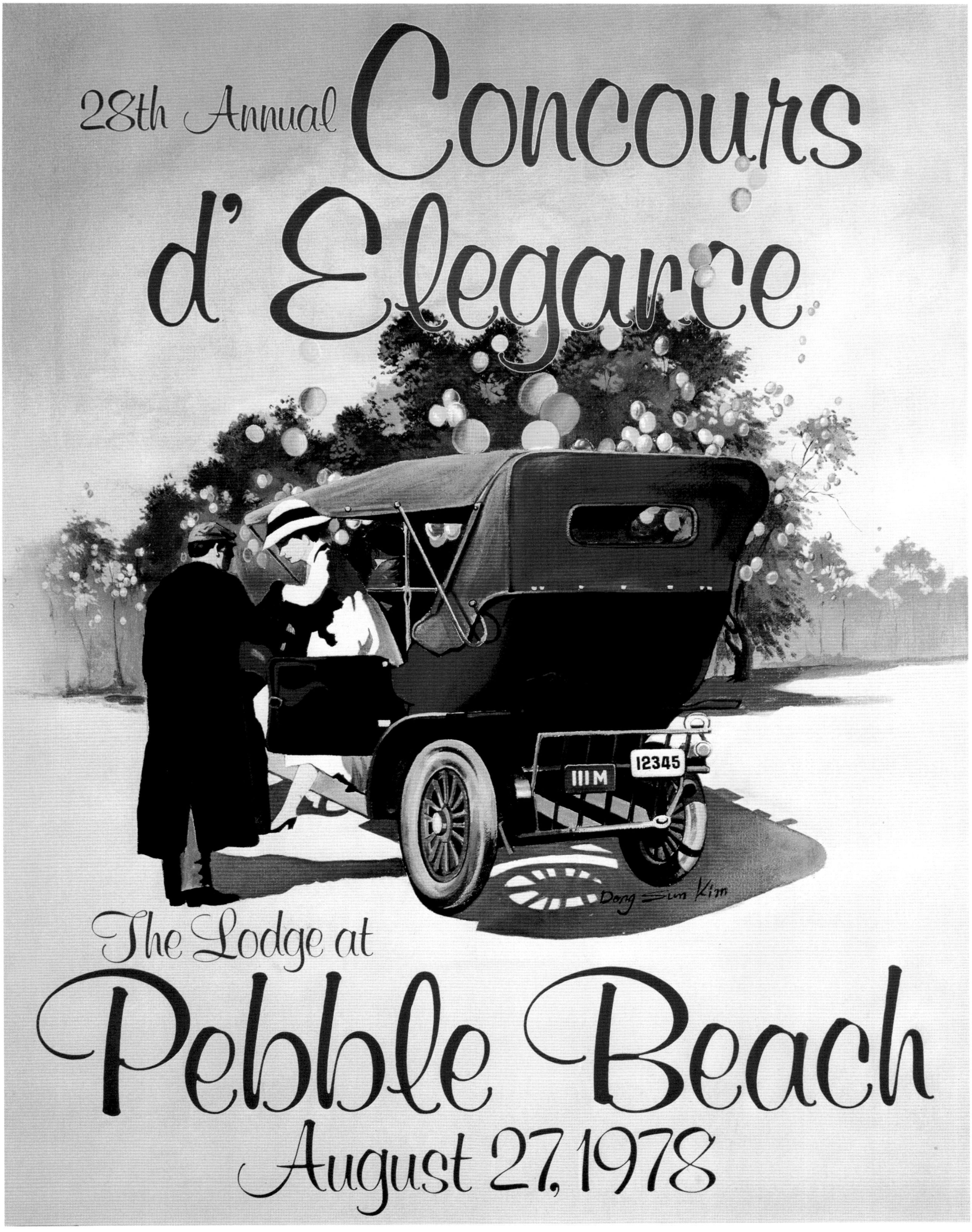
28th Annual Concours d' Elegance
12345
111M
Dong Sun Kim
The Lodge at
Pebble Beach
August 27, 1978

1979 Hank Ketcham

■ MUCH OF THE WORLD KNOWS HANK KETCHAM AS THE CREATOR OF THE "DENNIS THE Menace" cartoon strip, but regular participants of the Pebble Beach Concours d'Elegance know that Ketcham also loved cars—particularly cars with style. In 1979, Hank Ketcham agreed to do the Concours poster. He also served as an Honorary Judge at the Concours from 1979 to 1990.

On the poster, Ketcham has sketched a front view of a classic Rolls-Royce tourer—a Silver Ghost or a Phantom I, perhaps. The marque's distinctive radiator shell and grille with headlights, front bumper, and running lights are all outlined, and the car has been given dual side-mounted tires and side mirrors, which poke out from each side of the rakish windshield to provide a symmetrical image. The intertwined Rs of the Rolls-Royce symbol on the radiator have been replaced by the initials "PB" for Pebble Beach. But the Flying Lady mascot is nowhere to be seen! Instead Ketcham has balanced a jolly couple on the tip of the radiator. They are dressed ready to party, the taller lady in a flapper era outfit and the shorter man in full morning coat and top hat and sporting a bushy mustache. He has one arm around the lady's waist and in the other hand he holds a glass of champagne.

Behind them the graphics announce the Concours.

A single bold background color is used on the upper two thirds of the poster, accenting the merry couple and the text. Three versions of the poster were printed, using three different rich and distinct background colors: French blue, cranberry red, and vivid burnt orange. The poster is simplicity epitomized, but exciting and attention-grabbing.

A native of Seattle, Washington, Hank Ketcham was exposed at an early age to cartooning; a friend of his family drew "Moon Mullins," "Andy Gump," and "Barney Google." Ketcham determined to follow suit and eventually went to work as an animator for Walter Lanz, the creator of Woody Woodpecker, and then for the Walt Disney Company, applying his talent to the animated films *Fantasia, Pinocchio,* and *Bambi.* He spent World War II drawing military and propaganda posters. After his move to Carmel, he worked as a freelance artist and cartoonist, and his work appeared in *The Saturday Evening Post, Ladies Home Journal,* and *The New Yorker,* to name but a few publications. The "Dennis the Menace" strip was inspired in 1950 when Ketcham's wife reputedly burst into his studio to complain about their four-year-old son, Dennis, and shouted, "Your son is a menace!" Ketcham later pursued his interest in portrait and landscape painting, and his work has been displayed in many local institutions. His charitable good works and contributions were many in number, and on his death in 2001 at the age of eighty-one the flags in Monterey were flown at half mast.

Ketcham received many awards during his career, among them the coveted Reuben Award given by the National Cartoonists Society.

The artist's distinctive signature appears in the bottom right corner of the 1979 poster.

The original artwork, with acrylics on poster board, measures 20 by 40 inches.

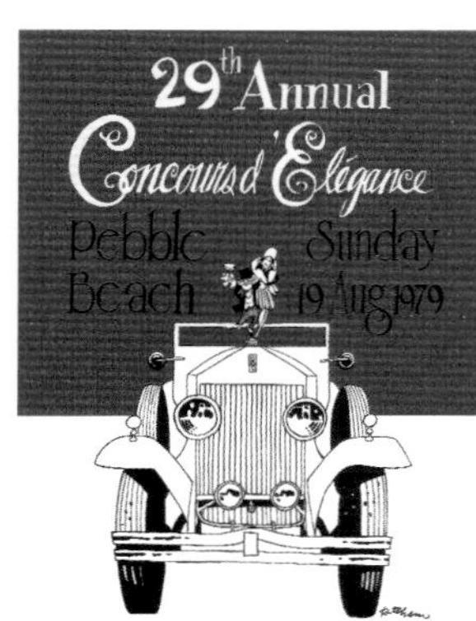

29th Annual
Concours d'Elégance
Pebble Beach
Sunday
19 Aug 1979
Ketcham

1980 Dick Cole

■ Five years after creating his first poster for the Pebble Beach Concours d'Elegance in 1975, artist Dick Cole returned to create the 1980 poster.

His second poster again features the front three-quarter profile of a car, but on this occasion, the car is a Duesenberg roadster. The great long hood of this car is accented by the sweep of its front fender line, and Cole has chosen to emphasize this expanse in his drawing. This particular Duesenberg is a pre–skirted-fender model.

Cole has focused on other details as well. The white sidewalls and wire wheels are immediately prominent. And the car's signature headlights, dual trumpet horns, and bumper lead the eye to the V-shaped radiator surround and the stylized Duesenberg hood ornament atop the radiator cap. Smaller side lamps are mounted near the belt course line on the cowl just above the side-mounted spare tire.

As the image recedes into the background, details become more muted.

Depth of field is also distinguished by the darkening shades on the fairway and the hills and sky—the more distant, the darker.

The highlights on the car and the long shadows cast by the trees indicate a late afternoon sun is shining off the sea.

30th
PEBBLE BEACH
CONCOURS d'ELEGANCE
August 24 1980
The Lodge at Pebble Beach

1981 Jim Miller

■ ARTIST AND WELL-KNOWN ILLUSTRATOR JIM MILLER CRAFTED THE PEBBLE BEACH CONCOURS POSTERS FOR BOTH 1981 and 1982.

Although born in Arkansas, Miller moved with his family as an infant to Southern California. He first studied engineering at California State College, but unhappy with his chosen career and attracted to art and illustration, he transferred on graduation to what is now the Art Center College of Design in Pasadena, California. During the next three years he worked in a wide range of mediums, developing his signature method of quickly drawing black-and-white sketches and then adding color. In his final semester he was awarded the prestigious Gold Medal from the Society of Illustrators of New York.

Over the years, Miller established a solid reputation in the art world, designing and illustrating advertisements, articles, and other printed publications for such companies as Universal Pictures, Continental Airlines, and *Road & Track* magazine. He served as the President of the Society of Illustrators of Los Angeles from 1972 to 1973. He has since opened his own art gallery in Carmel where he exhibits his paintings and lithographs, and his work is included in the collections of The White House, Wells Fargo, and many other national and international clients.

A very stylish 1930 Cadillac V-16 452 Rollston Convertible Coupé owned by Zach Brinkerhoff Jr. dominates the upper two-thirds of Miller's 1981 Concours poster. Drawn at a slight angle and facing to the left, all the essential features of the car are sketched in, from the massive headlights to the three wipers on the low, narrow windshield. Dual uncovered side-mounted spare tires are topped with side mirrors, and the running lights, the sidelights on the fenders, and the dual trumpet horns are all detailed. Too often, an artist can become distracted by the details of the radiator and grille of a car. Miller avoids this by presenting this area abstractly, using a series of dots and open areas that keep the eye moving toward the more dynamic features of the car, including the winged goddess mascot atop the radiator cap, and the gleaming hood. For the most part, the tires are left to the viewer's imagination, so as not to distract from the overall appearance of the car.

The reflections that are mirrored in blue, yellow, and green on the side and top of the hood bring the image to life, while the details of the hood vents give a sense of proportion. This is particularly important since there is no background in the picture to provide perspective. The lack of background does serve, however, to keep the viewer's attention on the car.

Three smaller images appear below the Cadillac. Sketched across the page are an Auburn Boattail Speedster, a Bugatti Type 57, and a Ferrari TRC. These three vehicles, along with the Cadillac, represent some of the best examples of design from the prewar years through the mid-1950s.

A single black line drawn around each sketch unifies the four pictures into one single stunning image, and the artist's signature appears on this line to the right.

The original artwork for the 1981 poster, a combination of pen and ink with dyes on heavy watercolor paper, measures 18 by 24 inches. The artist initially retained this artwork but later sold it.

31st pebble beach

concours d'elegance

august 23, 1981

the lodge at pebble beach

1982 Jim Miller

■ Jim Miller's second consecutive poster for the Pebble Beach Concours d'Elegance is a very detailed and elaborate montage of images. The medium is a pen-and-ink sketch, colored with red, pink, and blue acrylics.

As with his illustration for the previous year, one special car dominates the picture. This time it is the magnificent 1901 Panhard et Levassor 24 hp Clement Rothschild Touring car owned by George Wingard of Eugene, Oregon, which won the Antique Class at the 1980 Pebble Beach Concours. This is not a streamlined, sleek modern vehicle but transportation in transition, as metal, wood, wicker and glass mutate from the horse-drawn carriage of the nineteenth century to the automobile of the twentieth.

The two gleaming brass headlamps lead the eye to the uncovered radiator with its many coils, and then to the hood, which is hinged and louvered to control the flow of air to the engine. The car's narrow body widens out at the passenger section where the seats are richly upholstered in rolled leather. Note the wooden wheels on solid rubber tires and the wicker basket astride the rear fenders affording limited storage for an outing or picnic.

Three smaller automobile images surround the Panhard et Levassor—a Bugatti grille, the rear view of a 1930s grand limousine, and a Series One Ferrari GTO—providing a sweeping overview of the changes in vehicle design and style in the twentieth century. Blended into this collage is a beautiful lady wearing an elegant sunbonnet, and next to her, a nattily dressed modern gentleman, adjusting his sunglasses as if he was preparing to take the wheel of one of the illustrated vehicles. Both people stare directly at the viewers, seeking to catch their gaze and draw their attention to the surrounding scene.

In this poster, Miller has introduced some small background details to suggest the Pebble Beach setting. A pair of cypress trees and the striped roofs of the concession tents give depth and perspective. The repetition of multicolored stripes in the tents, the background, and the lady's hair and hatband unifies the entire poster.

Miller's signature appears near the lower right corner of his illustration.

The original artwork for the 1982 poster measures 18 by 24 inches. The artist initially retained this artwork but later sold it.

32nd Pebble Beach Concours d'elegance

august 22, 1982 • the lodge at pebble beach

1983 Thom Thomas

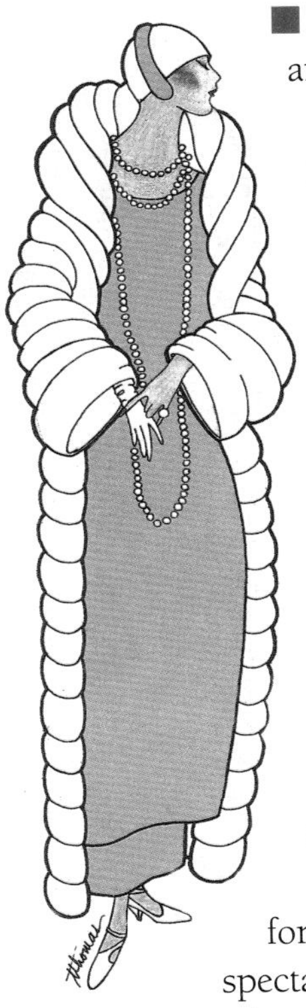

■ LOCAL ARTIST THOM THOMAS WAS COMMISSIONED TO PRODUCE BOTH THE 1983 AND 1984 POSTER art for the Pebble Beach Concours.

Thomas graduated from the School of Visual Arts in New York, where, in his formative years, he worked as a freelance fashion illustrator. He moved to Monterey in 1982, setting up his own company, Thomas & Thomas, and attracting contracts with several major companies. His published work in the early 1980s included the Thomsville Zoo Collection series, a record album cover for RTC Management, and the ABC computer book for children, *Alphabytes*.

For the 1983 Concours poster, Thomas created an attractive time warp of sorts—a piece with accents of art deco to depict the era of the late 1920s and early 1930s.

His artwork is dominated by the statuesque and highly fashionable woman on the left. Her body length has been slightly exaggerated from the waist down to give her the height to carry the ankle-length, multilayered French-blue gown. The formfitting white cloche on her head has a band of matching blue, and her eye shadow repeats the color. Her elegant white coat with its many horizontal rounded folds, which appears to be of Arctic fox, is also full-length. She is wearing a strand of pearls that are wound twice around her extended neck and fall to below her waistline. She is also wearing only one white glove, which allows the artist to show the pearl ring on her left pinkie finger.

To the woman's right, a Concours scene is encased in a blue and red border. In the foreground are three steps that lead upward to a chauffeur-driven phaeton admired by stylish spectators. The very blond woman on the steps is wearing a red-accented blue blazer the same hue as the border. Her knee-length white pleated skirt is further accented by the red color of her shoes and her scarf as it flows out and over the border. Thomas has added pattern and color to the clothing of the other spectators to enliven the scene. Such accents include a fox stole, ascot, bow tie, and era-related hairstyles—all of which lend to the mood of the poster. The chauffeur is in livery blue with matching cap, attending to the vehicle.

The towering pine trees are strikingly illustrated in brown and green against a wash of blue sky. The small yellow lemon tree in the lower right corner is an attractive element of the poster, with one lemon having fallen to the ground. Graphics in black are applied above and below.

The motorcar depicted is of a rather generic style, unidentifiable as any particular marque. However, in hindsight, it is interesting to note that the Best of Show for 1983 was in fact a very stylish 1930 Isotta Fraschini Tipo 8A SS Castagna Dual Cowl Phaeton, not unlike the car depicted in the poster. Could it be that Thomas had a vision of the winning car when he sketched his poster, several months before the show?

The artist's signature appears near the right foot of the statuesque woman.

33RD PEBBLE BEACH

CONCOURS D'ELEGANCE

THE LODGE
AT PEBBLE BEACH
AUGUST 28,1983

1984 Thom Thomas

■ A LIGHT AIRY TOUCH IS USED BY THOM THOMAS ON HIS SECOND CONSECUTIVE Concours poster.

Just the top half of a chauffeur-driven opera car is shown crossing the foreground from right to left. Thomas has used muted primary colors to capture the simple elegance of the vehicle. A rich brick red on the car body is matched with a brown landau leather top, both accented in gray and eggshell white to provide detail to the bright chrome and interior surfaces. Just the peak of the front fender and the upper third of the side-mounted spare tire are shown.

Seen through the circular porthole window is a sophisticated lady with a lace veil over her upper face.

The two figures in the lower left are dressed in clothing appropriate to the vintage of the featured automobile. The woman wears a yellow shirt to match her blond hair, a blue and white skirt below a vested top with tie, a fur stole, and white gloves. The gentleman, with his hands in his pockets, wears a white shirt and pants, a brown jacket, and a broad-brimmed hat and bow tie.

Interestingly all four of the characters portrayed in the picture lack eyes. Thomas interprets these faceless participants in his poster art with a similar whimsical approach to that of the actual physical location, and the anonymous nature of the featured motorcar.

If it were not for the European style of headlamps he drew, one could again easily assume Thomas had some prior knowledge of the Best of Show, long before it was chosen that year—a unique 1929 Cunningham V5410 All Weather Cabriolet with side mounts identical to those on Thomas' car.

An idyllic scene is depicted behind the opera car, with elements of the green fairway and interwoven pine trees in two shades of green interspersed to provide some depth of field. Additional perspective is added by Thomas' abstract of sea and shore that undulates across the background. Stillwater Cove is shown in reverse orientation.

The three red-and-white striped concessionaire tents add bright vertical elements while the multicolored balloons bring a festive ambience to the scene, which is surrounded with a colorful border.

Two items of whim are the twin gulls flying into the scene from the upper left and the single bright red balloon to the far right that has just made its escape from its mooring. These items extend beyond the colorful frame and give a sense of depth and dimension to the work.

Textual graphics are gathered at the bottom of the poster, which has a light gray border. Thomas' signature appears in the border to the right of his illustration.

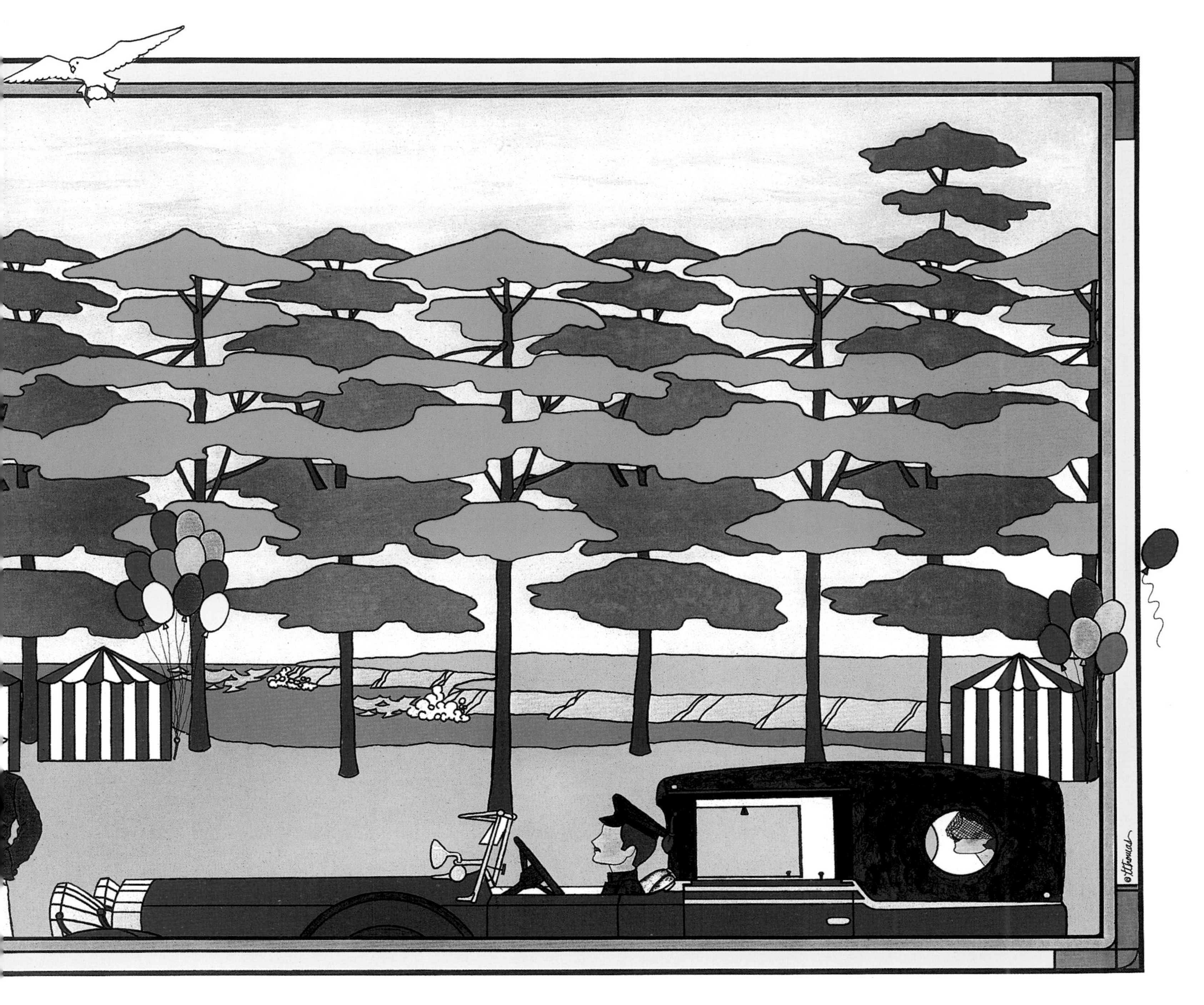

BLE BEACH CONCOURS d'ELEGANCE

THE LODGE · AT PEBBLE BEACH · AUGUST 26, 1984

1985 Loralee Lyman

■ The year 1985 is often referred to with more than a bit of reverence in Concours circles. That is the year the Pebble Beach Concours d'Elegance mounted an historic exhibit that established its reputation as the automotive show of shows.

The featured marque that year was Bugatti, and to mark the occasion Concours organizers decided to do something that had never been attempted, something that almost everyone said couldn't be done. They determined to unite all six of Ettore Bugatti's masterworks, his beautiful Bugatti Royales. Never before had all six cars been together, and to this day, they have not been reunited since their time together on The Lodge lawn.

This exhibition began in the imagination of Jean-Paul Caron, a well-established French photographer and author. It was his can-do attitude, along with the hard work of Concours organizers and a multitude of others, that squired the concept from whim to reality.

Everyone was awestruck.

It was local graphic designer and artist Loralee Lyman who was awarded the honor of creating the artwork for the poster and program cover for this historic occasion.

Lyman is a native of the Monterey area, having been raised on a ranch in Salinas. Drawing was among her favorite pursuits dating back to her days in a high chair. From these early beginnings, Lyman later pursued graphic arts in high school. She eventually went to work first for CAREX Resource Center and then for McGraw-Hill, where she enjoyed the distinction of being the youngest assistant art director in the company's history. She later attended the Fashion Institute of Design in San Francisco prior to returning to Monterey where she worked for five years for R.J. Wecker Graphic Design Company before starting her own design firm, Flipside Design, currently in its twentieth year.

In early 1985, shortly after she had established her own design business, Lyman received a call from one of the Concours' organizers, Carol Rissel, requesting her ideas for the 1985 poster. She submitted a pencil sketch not ever having seen a Bugatti let alone one of the Royales. She also began to research her subject with Rissel's assistance. Her drawing was ultimately accepted, and at age twenty-four, she became not only the youngest poster artist for the Pebble Beach Concours, but the first female. At the time, she was not aware of the prestige associated with the event, but she was happy to be selected.

Perhaps sensing that the grandeur of a Bugatti Royale could not be conveyed on paper, Lyman took a decidedly minimalist approach to what is a massive luxury car. She tucked a fairly small image of a Royale in one corner of the poster and surrounded it with space, creating a poster with simple elegance and style. Her specific automotive subject is Bugatti Royale prototype chassis 41100, drawn with simple evocative strokes and colored magnificently. This 1927 Coupé de Ville designed by Jean Bugatti, with body by Henri Binder, is known as the "Coupé Napoleon." It was brought across the sea from the Musée National de l'Automobile de France, in Mulhouse, France.

Lyman not only drew this Royale, she designed all of the graphics on the poster and she supervised every aspect of the printing process. She was among the first to use metallic inks mixed with Pantone inks; the former adorned the wheels and highlighted the beautiful shape of this Bugatti.

At the 1985 Concours, Lyman herself finally saw the Coupé Napoleon for the first time. She viewed it from all angles, even kneeling down to check the undercarriage, to be sure she had it right on the poster.

Lyman signed the 1985 poster in the lower right corner of her illustration. The original artwork, a pen-and-ink drawing which remains in Lyman's possession, measures 5 by 12 inches.

GE AT PEBBLE BEACH □ AUGUST TWENTY·FIFTH NINETEEN EIGHTY·FIVE

1986 Ken Eberts

■ It was in 1986 that the Pebble Beach Concours d'Elegance first hosted an exhibition by the Automotive Fine Arts Society (the AFAS). The AFAS had been formed just three years earlier by a few artists who firmly believed that automobiles were a legitimate subject for fine art. Their first exhibition was a success, and it soon became an integral part of the Concours.

The Concours poster artist for 1986 was Ken Eberts, one of the founding members of the AFAS and, to this day, its president.

From quite early in his life, the automobile was Eberts' creative inspiration. Born in Bronx, New York, on July 4, 1943, he was raised in tenement housing; bricks, concrete, and asphalt surrounded him. The only visual relief came from the cars parked on the street. As a nine-year-old, he formed his own imaginary car company—Future Motors, featuring the Kent and Bonzer automobiles, for which he made brochures and models that he sold to neighbors.

In his teens he attended a special high school for music and art students, and then he headed west to what is now Art Center College of Design in Pasadena, California. There he studied under Strother MacMinn, who served for years as Chief Honorary Judge at the Pebble Beach Concours d'Elegance.

Upon graduation Eberts joined the Ford Styling Center as an apprentice, and then he moved to Lockheed Aircraft to design the interior of the L-1011 airliner. In 1968, he left his industrial design position to become a full-time automotive fine artist.

The poster that Eberts generated for the 1986 Concours could not have made a stronger statement. His highly graphic creation is the epitome of modern poster art—a masterful exhibition of contrasting colors and juxtaposed boldness and subtlety.

The featured marque at the 1986 Concours was Mercedes-Benz, so Eberts choose to depict the magnificent Mercedes 540K. The front of the automobile, set at just a slight angle, looms large in the foreground of this poster. The car is a dramatic black with bright chrome accents. Its radiator grille, radiator cap with tri-star emblem, massive headlights, and twin trumpet horns are all painted in meticulous detail, and the horns and headlights are situated so they reach forward, capturing the attention of the viewer.

Depth of field is further established by the receding line of the car's long hood, which slants back to the V-shaped twin windshield and dark top. Accompanying chrome accents on this portion of the car include side trim, flex exhaust outlets, twin side-mounted lights attached to the windshield frame, and landau bar.

Four black pine tree trunks, directly behind the vehicle, rise to a canopy that frames the background which is painted with soft shades of green, yellow, blue and gray. A few immature pine trees dot the fairway that leads to Stillwater Cove. More distant fairways, tree-covered hills, and mountains create a peaceful panorama. Eberts also applied the textual graphics on this poster, in bright red and yellow.

The original artwork for the 1986 poster, a combination of gouache and watercolor on illustration board, measures 18 by 24 inches. The artwork was sold to Ralph Gaden, a Dallas Mercedes-Benz dealer.

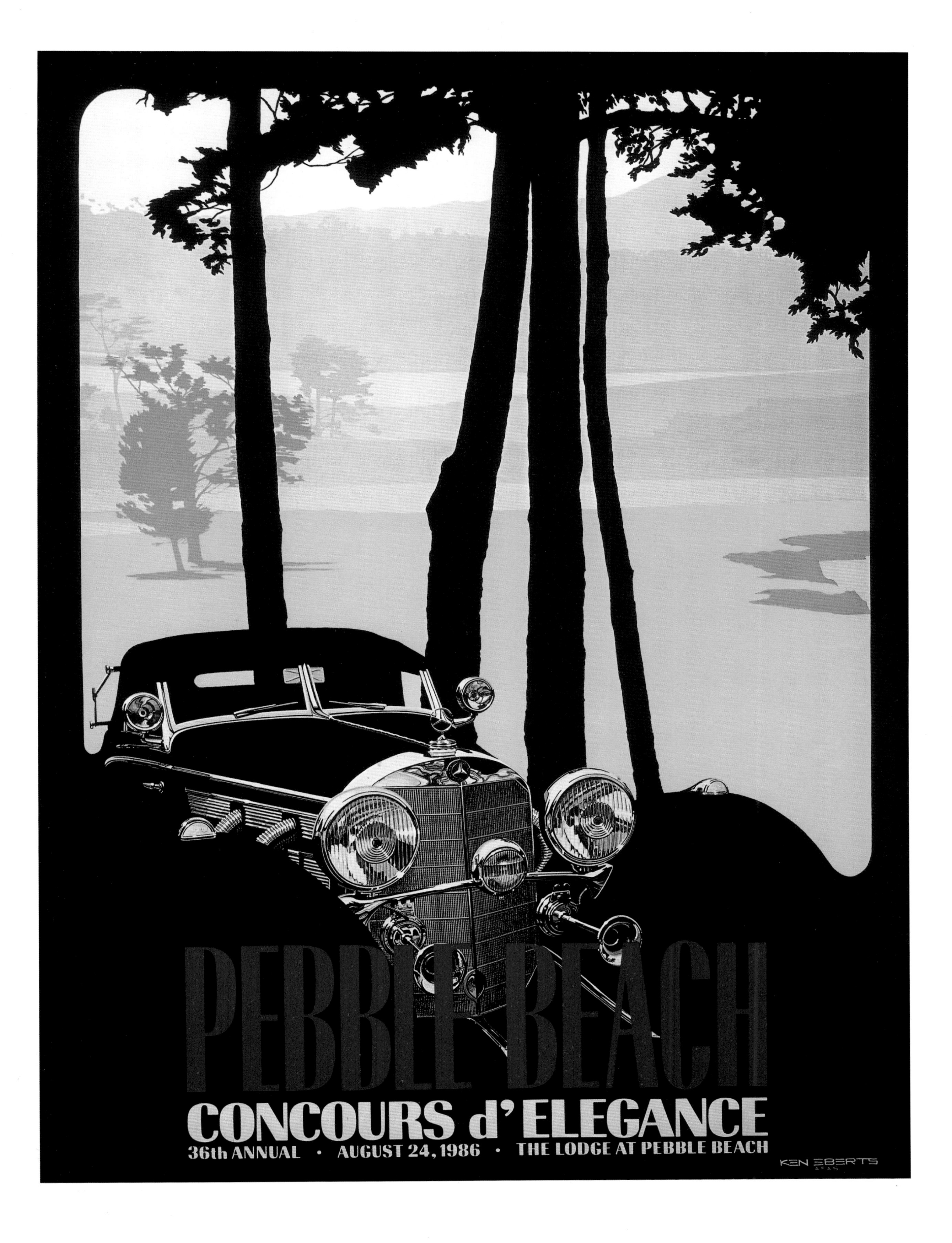
PEBBLE BEACH
CONCOURS d' ELEGANCE
36th ANNUAL · AUGUST 24, 1986 · THE LODGE AT PEBBLE BEACH
KEN EBERTS

1987 Ken Eberts

■ IN HIS SECOND SUCCESSIVE YEAR AS THE CONCOURS POSTER ARTIST, KEN EBERTS DEMONSTRATED VERSATILITY. Having made a bold statement in 1986, he shifted to a more muted color palette and an evocative style in 1987.

When he set to work, the featured marque had not been finalized, so he created a stylized dream car of his own—a car combining features of a Cord L-29 and a Bentley 8 Litre.

The car is situated in the background rather than the foreground of the 1987 poster. It is there to set the tone of the occasion; it is there for style. Even so, the car is presented with great attention to detail. It is an early 1930s two-tone roadster with large whitewall tires on chrome wire wheels. Note the lack of running board, the low windshield, and the cut down top of the rear-hinged suicide door. And note the dapper young owner's faithful dog poised waiting. Though dressed in a white three-piece suit, the owner strikes a casual pose with a topcoat over his left forearm, and a pipe in his gloved right hand.

In the foreground, an air of mystery is created—a slender woman stands with her back to the viewer. Her elongated figure is draped in a haut monde pink frock that falls in jagged tiers of fabric to mid-calf. She also wears a matching pink bonnet with puff.

The setting is minimal. Overlapping white scallops create a subtle sky to the upper left, and the outlines of tree trunks, limbs, and foliage appear in a neutral gray to the upper right. The same neutral gray serves as background for the scene as a whole, while a sweep of light demarcates a pathway from the car to the woman to the textual graphics, which are clustered in the lower left corner.

Three soft pastel colors—pistachio green, sunshine yellow, and pale rose pink—compose a tri-colored band that surrounds the scene.

Ken Eberts has signed the final poster in the lower right corner. Two early color roughs appear on this page, and the final poster follows on page 81.

The original artwork for the 1987 poster, a combination of gouache and watercolor on illustration board, measures 18 by 24 inches. The artwork was sold to Dick Barbour, the owner of a Le Mans–winning race car team.

37TH ANNUAL
PEBBLE
BEACH
CONCOURS d'ELEGANCE
AUGUST 23, 1987 • THE LODGE AT PEBBLE BEACH

1988 Ken Eberts

The third consecutive Pebble Beach Concours d'Elegance poster created by Ken Eberts is a highly stylized monochrome work, with tones ranging from light gray to black. Though muted, this piece is an effective depiction of the Pebble Beach Concours.

Hispano-Suiza was the Concours' featured marque in 1988, and Eberts depicts two of these cars on the poster. The cars have been parked at angles, so we see the front of one and the rear of the other. The marque's stork emblem is depicted on the radiator cap and on the trunk. The bumper, headlights, front tires, and wheels are also drawn in detail.

Sharing the foreground with these two cars are six well-dressed but slightly amorphous spectators, all attired for cold weather. Eberts has drawn these spectators with a subtle choreography of shade and contrast.

The setting is very clearly the Pebble Beach Concours d'Elegance; the full-length balcony of The Lodge at Pebble Beach serves as backdrop. Four double doors can be seen, each with fan-shaped windows overhead. At the railing, are two groups of spectators in conversation. The tents just in front of The Lodge provide shelter for Honorary Judges and Concours organizers during the event.

The black trunks of three pine trees, and the hint of foliage from one young pine to the far right, provide further context and depth of field.

The illustration has been given a frame that is black with two blue vertical stripes. The text appears in blue at the top and bottom of that frame.

Ken Eberts' signature appears in the lower right corner of the illustration.

The original artwork for the 1988 poster, a combination of gouache and watercolor on illustration board, measures 18 by 24 inches. As in 1987, the artwork was sold to Dick Barbour.

THE LODGE AT PEBBLE BEACH · AUGUST 21, 1988
KEN EBERTS AFAS
38TH ANNUAL
PEBBLE BEACH · CONCOURS D'ELEGANCE

1989 David Lord

THE YEAR 1989 WAS ANOTHER EXCITING YEAR FOR THE PEBBLE BEACH CONCOURS D'ELEGANCE; ALL THREE OF Nuccio Bertone's Alfa Romeo B.A.T.s (Berlina Aerodynamica Tecnica) were reunited on the ramp during the awards ceremony. The crowd was truly impressed, particularly when Bertone himself appeared with the cars.

For most of the day, the B.A.T.s were exhibited on the upper lawn of The Lodge, which is the setting of the 1989 poster. The poster was designed and painted by David Lord, a founding member of the Automotive Fine Arts Society.

Lord first went to Pebble Beach, with camera in hand, to photograph the site for his poster, and then he prepared a number of sketches and thumbnail drawings.

In the center of the final poster is the 1954 Alfa Romeo B.A.T. 7 Bertone-Scaglione Coupé, owned by Lorenzo Zambrano of Monterrey, Mexico, which went on to win the Briggs Cunningham Trophy in the Concours. Its bright silver color allows the car to act almost as a mirror, reflecting the surrounding scene. A masterpiece of the panel beater's art, these streamlined automobiles are a complete contrast to the elegant prewar cars normally seen at the Concours. To emphasize this difference, in the background of the poster, a stately black and red Isotta Fraschini points its nose toward the entrance of The Lodge. This poster was the first one to depict the entrance to The Lodge; other illustrations had the lower lawn or eighteenth fairway as their setting.

The mainly horizontal lines of the scene are offset on the left by a vertical frame of bright red bougainvillea, which creeps out and hides the rear fins of the B.A.T. but gives the poster the necessary visual impact. It is interesting to note that no people have been included to distract the viewer's attention away from the drama of the cars and the Pebble Beach setting.

David Lord has always been fascinated by automobiles. He remembers drawing them from an early age, with the encouragement of his father and grandmother. After studying advertising arts at the University of Hartford, he fulfilled a lifelong ambition and transferred to what is now the Art Center College of Design in Pasadena, California, where he earned a Bachelor of Fine Arts in industrial design. He states, "That was where I had to go. . . . They drew and designed cars there!" Following employment in the industrial design department of Uniroyal in South Bend, Indiana, he opened his own firm, which he operated for ten years before refocusing his energies into creating automobile fine art. In 1982, he was invited to exhibit at the Meadow Brook Hall Concours d'Elegance, where he met the other artists who ultimately founded the AFAS.

Lord's signature appears in the darkened foreground of the poster alongside the bougainvillea. The original artwork for the 1989 poster measures 30 by 40 inches and was sold at auction to Don Williams at the Blackhawk Collection.

THIRTY-NINTH ANNUAL

PEBBLE BEACH CONCOURS d'ELEGANCE

AUGUST 20, 1989 • THE LODGE AT PEBBLE BEACH

1990 Eldon Dedini

■ FOR THE FORTIETH ANNIVERSARY OF THE Pebble Beach Concours d'Elegance, cartoonist Eldon Dedini agreed to reprise his role as poster artist.

He set to work initially with two images in mind—that of a favorite car and a fantasy couple.

The car, placed at the center of the 1990 poster, is a Duesenberg phaeton, similar in many ways to the car depicted on Dedini's 1969 poster. Here again he has painted the car a deep French blue, and he has detailed it with proper radiator grille and mascot, raised running board ribs, and wire wheels.

Dedini's fantasy couple comprises an older man and a curvaceous younger woman. On the finished work, the gentleman is seen standing confidently erect, hands in pocket, the picture of modish old wealth. He is wearing a blue turtleneck sweater inside a brass-buttoned dark blazer and slacks, and a camel overcoat hangs casually from his shoulders in the best Continental style. The woman is seen leaning into the man, and her leg is specifically positioned so we can see the Duesenberg's front right wheel and fender. The woman's Rubenesque figure is clothed in a multicolored full-length dress with slit. A fur stole protects her from the chilly wind that is blowing her hair. She also wears a single strand of pearls around her neck and pearl drop earrings.

An elegant picnic is underway behind the car, and it is peopled with characters Dedini has pulled from many sources. An image in *Paris Match* inspired the mystery woman, and the satyr is often seen in his work for *Playboy*. The pretty young coquette on the picnic blanket seems overly interested in the main male character and is oblivious to the musicians that surround her. In addition to the satyr, those musicians include a girl cellist in flowing Greek tunic and an entertainer with mandolin. A peacock adds color in the foreground.

Dedini says he placed a rotunda in the background "to add an element of class to the setting." At right and left, Monterey cypress trees frame the scene, and in the distance, thermal clouds rise heavenward. The remainder of the background adds both color and depth of field.

As a whole the image draws upon a lush palette of rich jewel tones—bright blues, greens, and magentas—and simultaneously features dazzling sunlight and deep shadow.

Dedini has signed the illustration in the lower right corner. The Concours' graphic designer added the text and frame.

The original artwork for the 1990 poster, done in watercolor with some acrylic paint, measures 36 by 24 inches. The printed poster is a full-color photo engraving.

40 TH
ANNUAL
PEBBLE BEACH
THE LODGE AT PEBBLE BEACH
OURS d'ELEGANCE
Eldon Dedini Dedini '90

Dedini
Dedini

1991 Jack Juratovic

■ ROLLS-ROYCE AND PIERCE-ARROW WERE AMONG THE FEATURED marques at the 1991 Pebble Beach Concours, and stylish examples are depicted on the Concours poster for that year. Entitled *An Anglo-American Affair,* this creation of automotive fine artist Jack Juratovic includes many subtle dualities.

Focus is quickly drawn to the romantic setting behind the arched window, where a debonair British gentleman leans over to kiss the lips of an American heiress. The shadow of the lovers projected on the wall behind them is reminiscent of film noir, which was popular during the 1930s. Juratovic says the window scene was inspired by a painting by Tito entitled *Qui Trop Embrasse* from the circa 1931 French publication *Quatre Proverbes.*

Two uniformed and highly disciplined chauffeurs stand attending their vehicles, seemingly oblivious to the engaging scene unfolding between their master and mistress. The chauffeurs, "like garden statues," are exaggerated in art deco style.

The Rolls-Royce on the left is the 1931 Continental Phantom II prototype by Barker & Company that once served as the personal car of Sir Henry Royce. Note that the license plate number is the same year as the Concours. On the right, the Pierce-Arrow displays the distinctive in-fender headlights that became synonymous with the marque. While technically accurate, Juratovic has drawn both vehicles with the same dreamy qualities as the romantic setting in the background, and the close proximity of the two vehicles allows the Flying Lady mascot on the Rolls-Royce to interact with the kneeling archer on the Pierce-Arrow—an interplay reflecting what is occurring between the romantic couple behind them.

The rendezvous takes place on a very dark night, and the only source of light is a mellow glow emanating from the uncurtained window. The branches and foliage of a tree frame the picture. Note the artist's repeated use of rounded shapes.

Jack Juratovic has had a long and varied career in the automotive world. He grew up in New York and Pennsylvania and now lives in Lake Orion, Michigan. After graduating from the Cleveland Institute of Art with a diploma in industrial design, he was a junior designer for two years at the Ford Styling Center, working side by side with Ken Eberts, a future fellow founding member of the Automotive Fine Arts Society. There he refined his ability to render while assisting in the design of trim items such as the grille texture on the four-door Thunderbird. After he took a year off to race a Jaguar E-type, he returned to work at Chrysler Styling, and later at William Schmidt Associates, a small independent design firm. With Jack Purcell, a former associate at Ford Styling, Juratovic then founded BORT Design, specializing in after-market products such as the Cobra Mustang II and the Hurst Oldsmobile T Top. Although financially successful in this venture, his artistic heart was elsewhere, and his early love of streamliner trains and highly styled automobiles led to a number of paintings that paired the two. With the encouragement of other automotive artists, he made "one of those midlife changes at age forty-one," electing to return to full-time artwork.

His art has since been published in *Automobile Quarterly, Road & Track, Automobile, Auto Week, Automobile Classique,* and *Classic & Sports Car* magazines. He received the prestigious Richard and Grace Brigham Award for his work as editor and art director of *Automotive Fine Art: A Journal by the Automotive Fine Arts Society.*

The original artwork for the 1991 poster, a mixed media water acrylic and casein on gessoed Masonite board, measures 30 by 40 inches. It was sold to Don Williams of the Blackhawk Collection.

41st Annual

PEBBLE BEACH

1992 William A. Motta

■ The flamboyant art deco French automobile Delahaye was the featured marque at the 1992 Pebble Beach Concours, and its dramatic styling gave the well-known artist Bill Motta a wonderful opportunity to demonstrate his skills as a poster designer. He did not disappoint!

He initially submitted three or four rough poster ideas to the organizers of the Concours—Lorin Tryon, Jules "J." Heumann, and Sandra Kasky—and after some discussion, he went to work designing this dramatic, eye-catching scene. The flowing curves of the Delahaye, shown from its best angle, the rear view, are echoed in the dress and scarf of a sophisticated lady as she stands gazing out to sea, holding on to her wide-brimmed hat against the gentle breeze. Two Borzois, or Russian wolfhounds, complete the picture. The muted reflections of the dogs and model's face are traced in the side panel and trunk of the car. The Lone Cypress has long been a symbol of Pebble Beach, and Motta incorporated this motif into his design, placing the tree on the edge of a cliff overlooking the sea at the top of the poster. Behind the tree, the setting sun is disappearing behind some clouds, and a wonderful rosy glow spreads over all.

The model for the poster was Jill Du Amarell, the marketing manager at *Road & Track* magazine where Motta was the art director for many years.

Bill Motta grew up in Southern California and began his study of art in high school, winning a competition to design a poster for the Empress Hotel on Vancouver Island, Canada. In 1953 he enrolled at the Art Center School in Los Angeles, which is now the Art Center College of Design in Pasadena. There he focused upon advertising art, frequently incorporating cars in his designs and illustrations. After graduation he worked for a while as a freelance artist, designing covers for the *California Sports Car Club* magazine, among other publications. He found himself drawn increasingly to the world of automobiles, and he eventually accepted a position as assistant art director and then, later, art director for *Road & Track* magazine.

It was at *Road & Track,* where deadlines were tight, that Motta developed his skills with acrylic paint. The short drying time of the paint makes accuracy essential, and there is little margin for error. His artwork has appeared in the magazine for many years and continues to delight the eye to this day.

Motta is a founding member of the Automotive Fine Arts Society (AFAS). The artist's signature appears in the lower right corner of the poster, just below the tail of one of the dogs.

The original artwork is 24 by 36 inches. It was sold to Don Williams at the Blackhawk Collection.

PEBBLE
BEACH
42ND ANNUAL
CONCOURS
D'ELEGANCE
AUGUST 23, 1992
THE LODGE AT PEBBLE BEACH

1993 Nicola Wood

■ A concours d'elegance is not purely, nor even primarily, a competition. It is a celebration of the classic car and all that it represents. It is about style and excellence. It is about freedom and dreams.

Artist Nicola Wood understands this. Her 1993 Pebble Beach Concours poster offers a vision of pleasure and paradise, fantasy and escape.

The poster depicts preparations for a romantic picnic alongside a magnificent automobile on the lawn of The Lodge at Pebble Beach.

The automobile is a 1931 Cadillac 452 V-16 Pinin Farina Boattail Speedster owned by Robert Lee of Reno, Nevada. During the 1993 Concours this car was part of a Pininfarina (as the company has been known since 1961) special display on the upper lawn of The Lodge. The right-hand-drive custom coachwork vehicle was originally created for a maharaja for his hunting expeditions. Features include a special covered rear compartment with a shooting platform, and twin oversized spotlights that allow the hunter to stalk his prey after sundown. Wood has wisely chosen to depict the rear three quarters of the car, which features not only the boattail but special details like twin taillight pods. The car's position also affords the viewer a glimpse of a cut-down door, a side-mounted spare tire, and split windshield.

The Cadillac is parked atop a gathered satin sheet in a very luxurious setting—the eighteenth fairway at Pebble Beach. The background depicts Arch Rock at the entrance to Stillwater Cove, the expansive white sand of Carmel Beach, the blue green of the Bay, and the headlands leading to Carmel Valley.

On display, in a carefree array near the car, are numerous items that establish the romantic mood: champagne in a bucket being chilled and two flutes ready for sampling, long-stemmed pink roses that have been strewn about, a pair of red slingback high heels that match the red trim on the car, and a broad-brim sun hat with flower and leopard hat band. Leopard is Wood's signature pattern, and her illustrations always include it.

The romantic couple is nowhere to be seen. Perhaps they are nearby—or perhaps the viewer is being invited to step into the fantasy.

Nicola Wood was born and raised in a rural setting in the north of England, with very little exposure to the arts or culture of any sort. Nonetheless, Wood knew at an early age that she was destined to be an artist. It was in the local movie theatre, the Odeon, that she witnessed another world—that of Hollywood, with its glamorous stars, swimming pools, and automobiles. These influences would later inspire her work; they would serve as the subjects of her oil paintings.

Wood first attended the Southport School of Art near Blackpool, and then Manchester Regional College of Art, where she earned her National Diploma in Design. She undertook three years of post-graduate studies at the Royal College of Art in London, earning a Master's Degree with First Class Honors, and she was then awarded a Fulbright scholarship to study at Parsons School of Design in New York City.

While attending Parsons, Wood landed her first, and very prestigious, commission, a book cover for Tennessee Williams' *Night of the Iguana*. Soon thereafter, she developed a series of four full-page advertisements for CBS that appeared in the *New York Times*.

Following her stint at Parsons, Wood briefly returned to England, starting her own business and teaching art classes two days a week some sixty miles away. She says she owned a Super 90 Porsche "which fit me like a glove. I exceeded the speed limit enthusiastically. I had a good time driving to and from the teaching assignment with my poodle, Kiki, who leaned into the curves and braced himself with his front paws."

Wood later moved to California, where she developed an obsession with the large-finned Cadillacs of the 1950s and 1960s. In her work, these Cadillacs and other chrome and pastel cars now often share center stage with pop cultural icons like the Radio City Rockettes dance line and pink flamingos.

Nicola Wood was invited to join the Automotive Fine Arts Society in 1988.

On the 1993 poster, Wood's signature appears in the lower right corner.

The original artwork for the poster, which is oil on canvas, measures 46 by 60 inches. It was sold to John and Robin Fuchs.

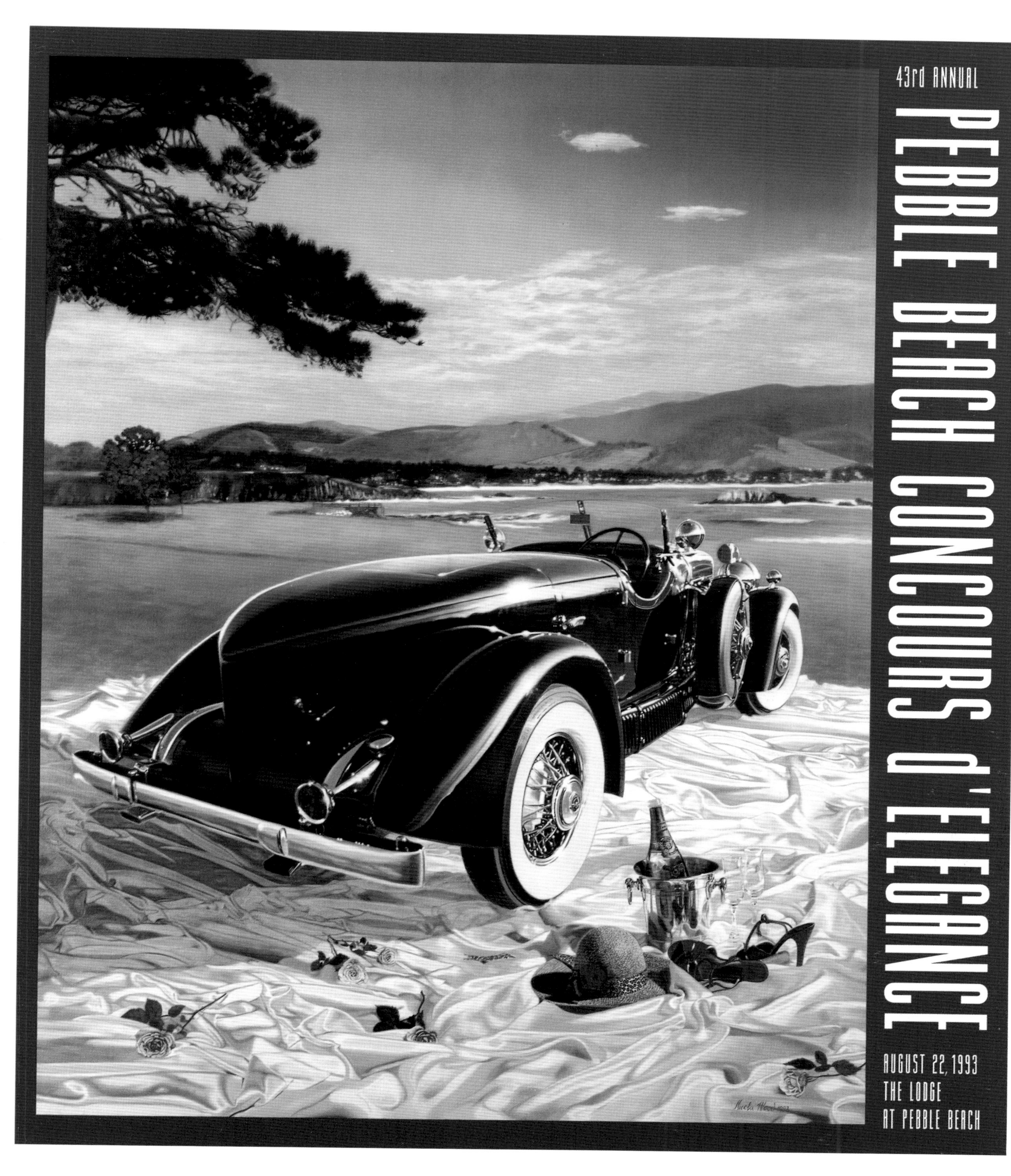
43rd ANNUAL
PEBBLE BEACH CONCOURS d'ELEGANCE
AUGUST 22, 1993
THE LODGE
AT PEBBLE BEACH

Nicola Wood 93

1994 Ken Eberts

■ TWO POSTWAR MARQUES—FERRARI AND PEGASO—WERE FEATURED AT THE 1994 PEBBLE BEACH CONCOURS d'Elegance, and automotive artist and AFAS president Ken Eberts was asked once again to design the poster to mark the occasion.

Eberts, who had previously created the posters for 1986 through 1988, choose two unusual automobiles as his subjects. The foreground of his poster shows the two-tone red-and-black 1953 Pegaso Z 102 B 2.8 Litre Berlinetta Touring car known as "Thrill." Owned by the Minasian family, the car went on to win its class at the Concours. In the background is the pale cream 1954 Ferrari 375 MM Pinin Farina Berlinetta Speciale built for Swedish actress Ingrid Bergman and featured at the 1954 Paris Salon. Owned by the Golomb Family Trust, this car was included in a special exhibit on the Concours' upper field.

Both cars were considered groundbreaking designs in the early 1950s. The Ferrari's scalloped recess behind the front wheel arches would become a Corvette trademark in 1956, and its tunnel-back inset rear window treatment was later seen on subsequent Corvettes and Ferraris.

Eberts has positioned the two cars with their backs together at a right angle on a swath of green. In the distance, providing depth of field and firmly establishing the specific setting of the Concours, Eberts shows Monterey pines and coastal rocks, the blue of Stillwater Cove, the distant sixth fairway of Pebble Beach Golf Links, the tree line of the foothills, and Pinyon Peak Lookout, located in Carmel Valley.

To provide added visual interest and establish the stylish nature of the Concours, Eberts includes the white outline of a well-dressed woman in a black panel that sweeps across the poster from the upper left to the lower right.

The image is framed in black and red, and textual graphics are grouped in the lower left corner. Eberts signature appears in the lower right corner of his illustration.

The original artwork for the 1994 poster, a combination of gouache and watercolor on illustration board, measures 30 by 40 inches. It was sold to Charles Cawley, then Chairman of the Board and now Chief Executive Officer of MBNA Corporation.

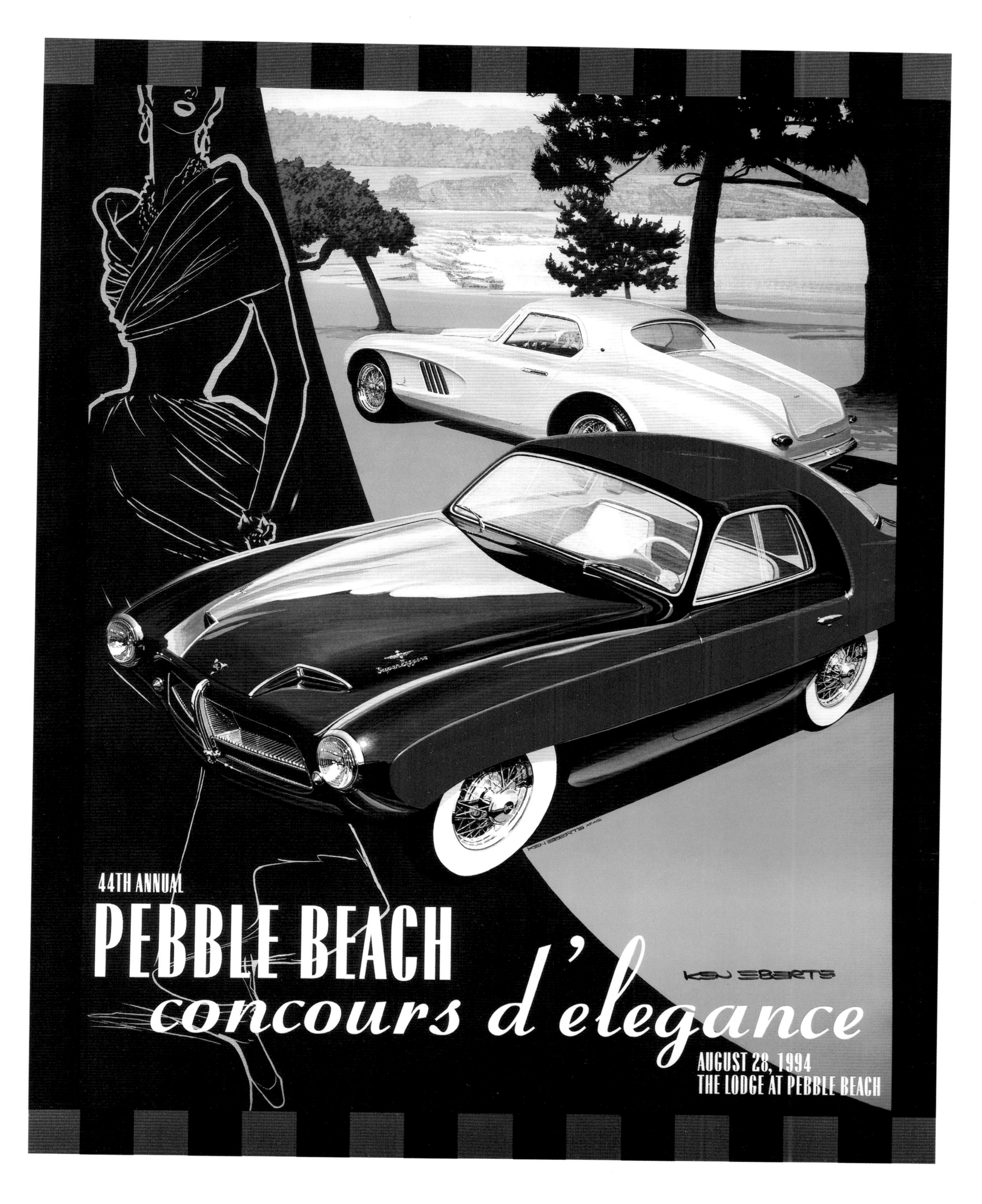
44TH ANNUAL
PEBBLE BEACH
concours d'elegance
KEN EBERTS
AUGUST 28, 1994
THE LODGE AT PEBBLE BEACH

1995 Dennis Brown

■ On the list of Best of Show winners at the Pebble Beach Concours d'Elegance, one name is repeated much more often than others—that of J. B. Nethercutt of Sylmar, California. Nethercutt has won the show's top award a total of six times, and his meticulous restorations have long set the standard for all others to follow. Nethercutt has also served the Concours as a Judge, and he is one of its most ardent supporters.

Accordingly, in 1995, the Concours saw fit to recognize J. B. Nethercutt's many accomplishments and contributions to the automotive world. It mounted a display of several of the cars in his prized collection, and the poster and program for the year were a tribute to him.

The 1995 poster art, created by artist Dennis Brown, features J. B. Nethercutt and his wife, Dorothy, in their 1929 Rolls-Royce Phantom II Brewster Town Brougham, which won Best of Show in 1992. Brown sets the Phantom at an angle in the circle drive at the entrance to The Lodge at Pebble Beach.

A famous Rolls-Royce Silver Ghost (registered as AX201) is depicted in the background. This car won the Dewar Trophy for its success in a 15,000 mile nonstop run, and it was later displayed at the 1907 Olympia Show in London.

Artist Dennis Brown is a native of the Los Angeles area. After serving in the U.S. Army, he attended California State University, Long Beach, and majored in art. He later studied at the Otis Parsons Art Institute of Los Angeles, and what is now the Art Center College of Design in Pasadena, California. During much of this time, to earn a living, he worked as a foreman at Schiefer Engineering, a producer of auto speed equipment.

His art career began with work as an architectural illustrator, and to this day, his artwork often includes structural settings and details. His "big leap ahead" occurred when *Road & Track* magazine hired him. There, art director William Motta served as his mentor, helping him develop his method and style.

Brown generally does an initial pen-and-ink drawing, and then he applies liquid color acrylics, gradually developing a three dimensional form that brings his illustrations to life. He finishes with a krylon crystal clear coating that adds a luster to his artwork. "I attempt to present my automotive subjects as if just freshly prepared for a Concours, gleaming and glittering with bright highlights and shaded surfaces."

Brown has done work for *Cavallino* and *Westways* magazines, and many leading automotive manufacturers. He also has worked with major media, advertising, and entertainment companies.

Brown now teaches at Mt. San Antonio College in Walnut, California, which, with some 40,000 students, is the largest community college in the United States.

Brown signed his 1995 poster in the lower right corner. His original artwork for the poster is now included in the Nethercutt Collection in Sylmar.

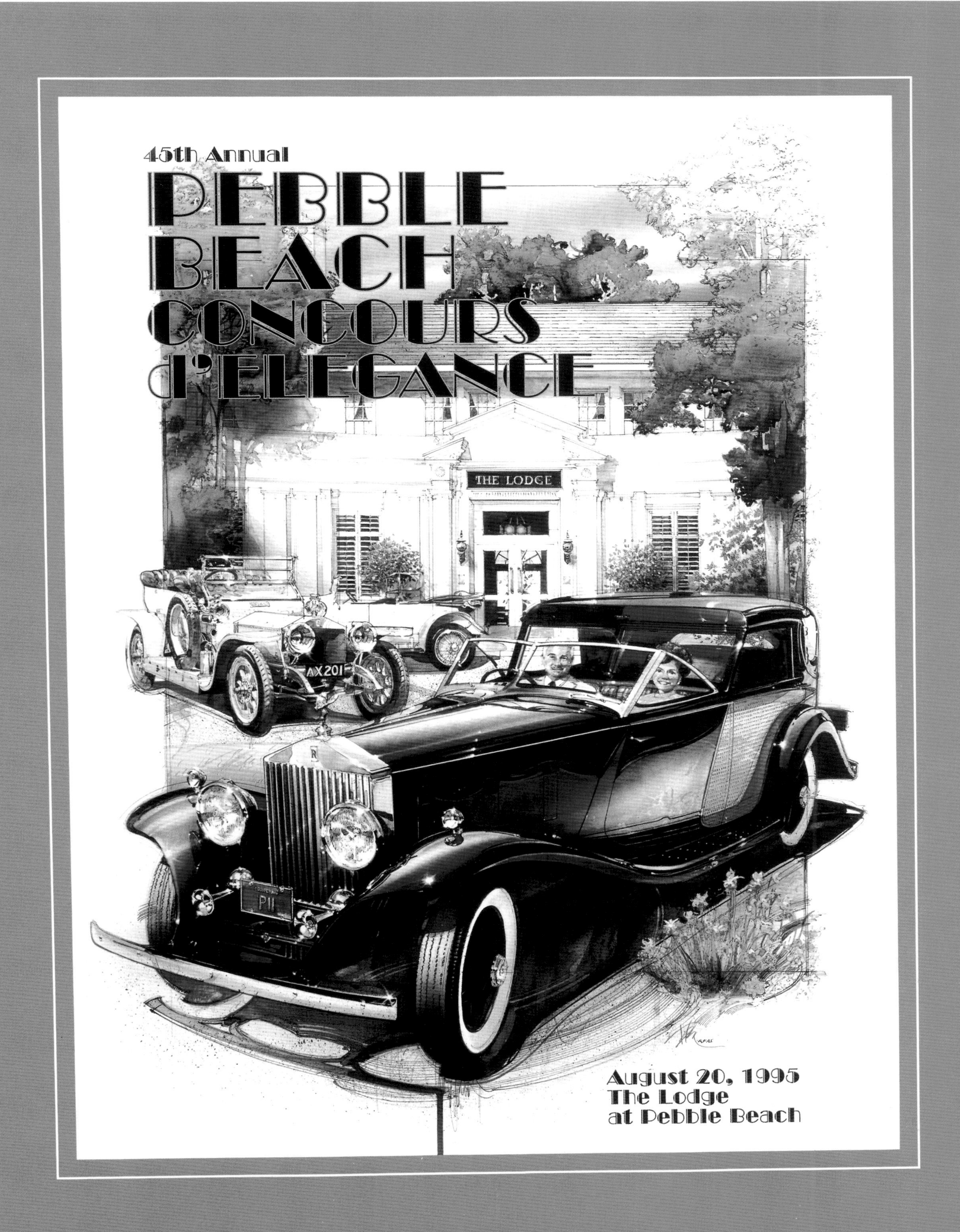
45th Annual
PEBBLE
BEACH
CONCOURS
d'ELEGANCE
THE LODGE
AX201
P11
August 20, 1995
The Lodge
at Pebble Beach

1996 Ken Dallison

■ A RAINBOW OF RICH COLOR IS SPLASHED ACROSS THE 1996 PEBBLE BEACH CONCOURS POSTER. CREATED BY artist Ken Dallison, the poster depicts the scene on the eighteenth fairway of Pebble Beach Golf Links on Concours Sunday.

The eye is immediately drawn to the angled Ferrari in the foreground with its deep blue paint and the bright green of the fairway reflected off its shiny wings. The Ferrari, a 1956 250 GT Berlinetta (serial number 0515GT), bodied by Zagato and owned by Ferrari collector Lorenzo Zambrano of Monterrey, Mexico, went on to win its class at the Concours. No doubt to celebrate, Mr. Zambrano also purchased the original artwork for this poster!

Behind the Ferrari and at a right angle to it is a stately chauffeur-driven 1927 Lincoln L Coaching Brougham by Judkins, owned for many years by William Harrah of Reno, Nevada, ablaze in contrasting bold yellow and black. Note that the chauffeur behind the wheel is conspicuously reading a newspaper!

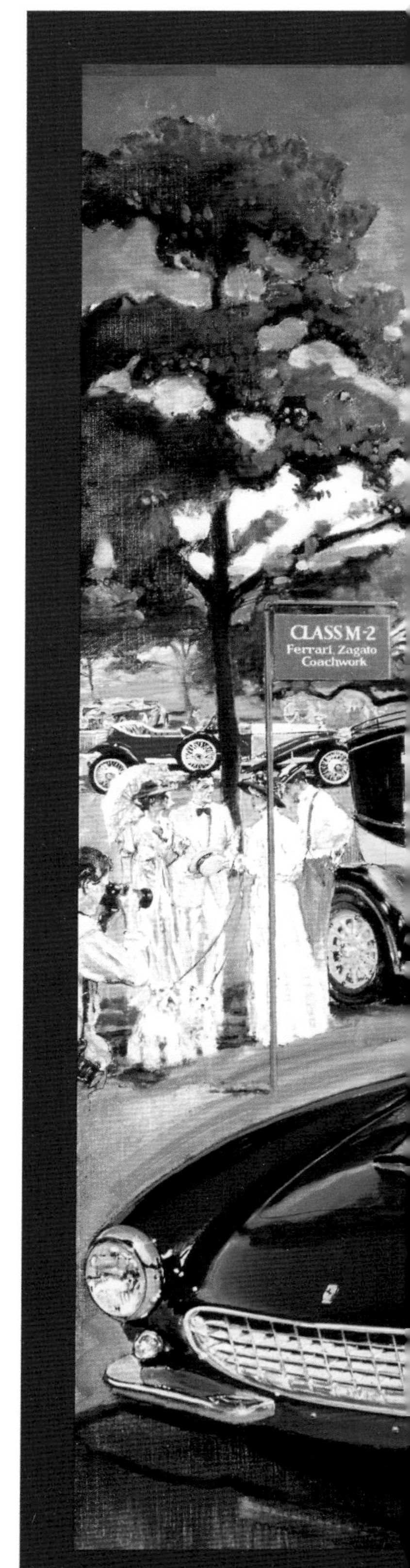

Close inspection of the background reveals among others, a green Delahaye, a pair of Rolls-Royce cars, a brown and pale yellow Auburn boattail, and a Duesenberg and a Mercedes-Benz both in red.

There is much activity in the poster but this does not disturb the leisurely mood. Most participants are smartly dressed except for the man opening the Ferrari door. One wonders if he is the detailer preparing to give the Ferrari its final dust and polish before the judging begins. The photographer at the left is capturing this activity On the edge of the picture, note the vintage period scene of ladies and gentlemen dressed in finery from the early twentieth century. In the right foreground, the artist has painted his wife, Gwen, attired in a red hat and standing with her cousin holding his English shooting stick. At anchor in Stillwater Cove is the 72-foot motor yacht Lycon owned by Gil and Beth Nickel of the Far Niente winery. The overall feeling is a relaxed and comfortable mood with the participants thoroughly enjoying a genteel outing on a glorious sunny day.

A lengthy look at the poster reveals innumerable details. For example, the Ferrari's front wheels are turned just slightly to the right to show off their detail, and the steering wheel is turned accordingly. This attention to detail is a hallmark of Dallison's work.

Ken Dallison grew up in England. He attended the Twickenham School of Art, just west of London, and the training served him well during his National Service when he was occupied as a cartographer. After moving to Ontario, Canada, where he now lives, he worked as an artist on a variety of freelance assignments.

In the United States his automotive artwork was first seen in the pages of *Car and Driver* magazine in the 1960s. Dallison considers this association and this period to be "my big development years." He has also designed artwork for *Sports Illustrated, Road & Track, National Geographic* and *Esquire* magazines. Other notable assignments include the design of a U.S. postal stamp celebrating the 100th anniversary of the automobile. In 1970 he was awarded the Gold Medal of the New York Society of Illustrators, and he has also been presented with a Lifetime Achievement Award from the Canadian Association of Photographers and Illustrators in Communications. He is a founding member of the Automotive Fine Arts Society.

The original artwork for the 1996 poster, which is oil on canvas, measures 40 by 28 inches.

PEBBLE

46TH ANNUAL

concours

AUGUST 18, 1996

d'elegance

THE LODGE AT PEBBLE BEACH

BEACH

1997 Nicola Wood

■ In 1997, the Pebble Beach Concours turned its attention to the steam car of old, to marques like Stanley, White, and Doble. And Concours organizers asked Nicola Wood to return as poster artist to illustrate these beauties. Wood had first created the 1993 Concours poster.

On this occasion, Wood takes viewers back to a very peaceful era.

In the foreground is one Stanley Runabout—in tomato red, with yellow wheels and black upholstery reflecting blue sky. Its large front brass lamps carry a high luster, showcasing Wood's skills. Brass was often used on luxury automobiles prior to World War I, when it was set aside for shell casings. Note the offset front seat, providing the driver with more legroom. A third "mother-in-law" seat is located in the far rear.

In the background, gaining steam, is a second black Stanley touring model, again with yellow wheels.

Two small pine trees help frame the illustration. In the background are Point Lobos on the left and Pescadero Point on the right.

There is just one person in this illustration—a woman who stands poised to the left, facing away from the viewer. She is wearing a long golden-apricot satin gown and she carries a long-stemmed rose in her hand and holds onto her sunbonnet so it is not carried off by the light breeze. Her parasol and binoculars are lying on a tasseled leopard print ground cloth. The woman's handsome Afghan hound stands nearby, seeming very relaxed.

Two seagulls appear in Wood's original painting, representing a love interest. Unfortunately, when the necessary textual graphics and frame were added for the poster, one of these seagulls was lost.

Wood's signature appears in the lower right corner.

The original artwork for the 1997 poster, created with oils on canvas, measures 40 by 52 inches. The artwork was sold to the owner of the red stream car.

FORTY-SEVENTH ANNUAL

PEBBLE BEACH

CONCOURS D'ELEGANCE

AUGUST 17, 1997

1998 Barry Rowe

■ MINERVAS TOOK TO THE FIELD IN NUMBERS AT THE 1998 Pebble Beach Concours, and they are featured prominently on that year's poster, the first by artist Barry Rowe.

With masterful use of light and shadow, Rowe transports viewers to a concours d'elegance where several of these Belgian-built cars are on display. The setting, with Monterey pines, Carmel Bay, and distant peaks, is clearly the lawn of The Lodge at Pebble Beach. But the era predates the Pebble Beach Concours d'Elegance; it is the era of the classic car.

From the left, the front end of a Minerva AKS Tourer pushes its way to the foreground of the illustration so the marque's signature mascot, the Goddess Minerva, is prominently displayed. At center, another Minerva—a dual cockpit cycle fender car—is featured.

A larger than life but very fashionable lady appears in the right foreground in a pale gold gown, gathered at the waist. She is adorned with a long strand of pearls wound around her neck and an art deco three-element pearl bracelet with extended strands, and she carries a translucent floral sun parasol. Other people are all dressed in period clothing and all wear broad-brimmed sun hats.

Rowe's brushwork adds an impressionist touch. Note the colors that he uses on the sky; while the sky peeping through the trees is blue, the sky below the tree line is painted an unusual light golden hue. This hue helps to separate the tree from the background and sea.

The illustration as a whole offers a vision of a different time.

Born and raised in Coventry, England, artist Barry Rowe was intimately exposed to the world of the automobile at an early age; his father worked at Jaguar when its C-types and D-types held sway in the racing world. In 1948, when the famed XK120 was introduced, the younger Rowe was immediately infatuated with it and he determined to draw it. At age ten, he had some difficulty mastering the shape, but he persisted until he felt his drawing was accurate.

As a teenager, he studied at the Coventry School of Art and Design and the Coventry College of Art and then he went directly to work in a studio and an advertising agency. By the age of seventeen, his work was being published, and by twenty, he was an art director, working with clients like fire pump and racing engine manufacturer Coventry Climax.

Through work, he met motoring photographer Edward Eves, and soon Rowe was painting covers for *Sporting Motorist.* Though he was not well paid, he received airfare and press credentials to attend the grand prix races to gather ideas for his cover paintings. His work was strongly influenced by leading automotive artist Gordon Crosby, who created covers and other artwork for *Autocar* magazine, and Walter Gotschke, who is best known for his pre- and postwar depictions of the German racing scene.

Rowe has been a freelance illustrator since 1966, but his career as a painter kicked into high gear in 1994 after he won Sotheby's Art Award for his portrait of five-time World Drivers Champion Juan Fangio. Since that time, he has received commissions from a diverse group of clients, including Louis Vuitton of Paris, Royal Mail, Royal Doulton, and Royal Caribbean Cruise Lines. And his work can often be seen in *Road & Track, Classic & Sports Car, Autoweek, Automobile Quarterly* and *Automobile Year.*

Rowe's signature on the 1998 poster appears in the lower left corner.

The original artwork for the poster measures 40 by 30 inches.

48th annual
PEBBLE BEACH
Concours d'Elegance
THE LODGE AT PEBBLE BEACH
AUGUST 16, 1998

1999 Barry Rowe

THE LATE 1990S WAS A TIME FOR PLANNING, A TIME TO NURTURE GREAT expectations. The Pebble Beach Concours d'Elegance would be marking its fiftieth anniversary in the year 2000, and Concours organizers wanted the celebration to be grand. But plans were suddenly upended with the death in 1999 of Lorin Tryon.

Tryon and Jules "J." Heumann had served for twenty-eight years as Concours Co-Chairmen, guiding the event to world-class status. Now the Concours needed new leadership at a crucial time.

Eventually, of course, a new team of leaders would evolve. By 2000, Heumann would move to the position of Chairman Emeritus but remain very active. Automotive enthusiast and retired businessman Glenn Mounger would step into the role of Chairman that year, and in 2002, Mounger would ask the event's longtime Executive Director, Sandra Kasky, to serve as Co-Chairman with him. A new Advisory Board was also established, and the new position of Chief Judge was ably filled by Ed Gilbertson.

The show would go on. And indeed it does.

The 1999 Concours poster, the second by Barry Rowe, honors the centennial of Packard.

A horizontal work, Rowe's painting features the long side profile of the 1934 Packard Model 1108 Dietrich Sport Sedan known as the "Car of the Dome." This Packard was originally displayed at the Travel and Transportation Building of the Century of Progress Exposition in Chicago in 1933. Initially, Rowe needed pictures of the car and Heumann passed some to him. Rowe then did some sketches and faxed them back to Heumann for comment. Word came back: the car was not quite right. Later, in conversation, the two men realized it was not Rowe's sketch that was the problem; the fax had distorted the image, compacting the car and squashing the tires flat.

At the outset, Rowe found the Packard's brown color to be a challenge. He brought the brown to life by adding reflections and highlighting the grass under the chassis. Posed sitting on the running board, wearing a colorful dress and flowered bonnet and reading a book, is Sandra Kasky's daughter, Sonja.

The Packard has a V-shaped shouldered radiator grille, headlights and split windshield, which are typical of the mid to late 1930s, as are the skirted front fenders and the large whitewall tires on wire wheels. The spare tire has moved from the front fender to the car's rear, so one clean long line sweeps along the side of the car, and that line is relatively high. Note that the car has rear-hinged suicide front doors and front-hinged rear doors; front and rear doors share the same external hinges on the center pillar.

In the background, is a red and black earlier Packard model, and injecting itself into the picture from the lower left corner is a Lagonda drophead with rear-hinged suicide door. Couples in period dress stroll among the vehicles, adding color to balance the painting's more muted automotive centerpiece. Rowe has taken some artistic license with the background, reversing and revising some of the geography of the setting. Pine trees grow out of rising grassy terrain to the right, and to the left, the headlands of Carmel Valley are visible, along with a narrow wedge of Stillwater Cove with several sailboats at play. Whiffs of clouds lace the otherwise picture-perfect blue sky.

Rowe's signature appears in the lower left corner of the painting.

The original artwork for the poster, which is acrylic on canvas, measures 30 by 40 inches. Its sale helped Concours charities.

The Lodge at Pebble Beach ~ August 29, 1999

2000 John Francis Marsh

■ ON THE OCCASION OF ITS FIFTIETH ANNIVERSARY, THE PEBBLE BEACH CONCOURS D'ELEGANCE GRANDLY MESHED past with present. A host of previous Best of Show winners returned to repose beside the waters of Carmel Bay, and several winning cars from the early Pebble Beach Road Races were on hand as well.

John Francis Marsh was asked to create the 2000 Concours commemorative poster—and he knew it had to be special. Rather than one marque or one moment, Marsh had to find a way to depict the full history of the event. It was an assignment that Marsh was uniquely suited to tackle. He is known for paintings that combine a multitude of images into one. His paintings do more than translate three-dimensional images into two; they collapse history—setting it forth for all to see. In automotive circles, Marsh is perhaps best known for the painting that depicts the design of the Volkswagen Concept 1 car that was the basis for the new Beetle.

Marsh is interested in the process of design—whether in creating a car or in planning a show like the Pebble Beach Concours d'Elegance. "People think the cars arrive, they pull into line, and the judges review them," says Marsh. "But the Concours is more than that. There's a planning process behind it. And that's what I've tried to paint."

Even as a child, John Francis Marsh wanted to be a designer. He pieced together model airplanes and automobiles from kits, and he created dream cars of his own. At age thirteen, he began to enter his designs in the Fisher Body Craftsman Guild Automotive Model Competition, sponsored by General Motors, and over the years, he won more than a few awards. Marsh went to what is now the Art Center College of Design, where he earned a Bachelor of Professional Arts degree with honors. Then he worked for General Motors Design Center and Sundberg-Ferar Industrial Design before establishing a successful industrial design firm in San Francisco with three other partners. Marsh had been advised while at Art Center, that he was a skilled painter, but it was not until 1972, that he began to shift his career toward full-time painting. Marsh now lives and paints in the Sierra foothills in a stone house of his own design and construction, commuting weekly to teach at Academy of Art College, San Francisco.

To create the Concours poster, Marsh initially layered transparent watercolors on paper and he used acrylic inks and washes to add brilliance and tonal depth. He then worked with opaque tempura watercolors to increase the range and intensity of colors and add finishing touches. The final poster is the result of eighteen months of hard work.

The poster depicts a room inside The Lodge at Pebble Beach, where preparations for the fiftieth anniversary of the Concours are underway. The setting is established by the view out of the window—the Concours' show field on the famed eighteenth fairway of Pebble Beach Golf Links.

At a desk in the upper right corner, Concours Executive Committee members Jules Heumann, Sandra Kasky, and Glenn Mounger meet to review plans for the 2000 event. The image of Lorin Tryon, the former Co-Chairman of the Concours, is there as well—in a frame on the desk. The image of Strother MacMinn, the Concours' Chief Honorary Judge for years and one of Marsh's mentors, appears in a frame atop a stack of books on a stool in the foreground.

It is the cars, appropriately, that really take prominence in the picture. A large painting depicts one of the Bugatti Royales that took to the field in 1985. And one of Bertone's B.A.T.s appears just to its right. Several Best of Show winners are displayed, and there are many other notable automobiles.

Marsh also manages to pay tribute to the work of several of his fellow artists. David Lord's poster sits at the edge of the table where the organizers are making plans. Two of Eldon Dedini's posters hang on the back right wall, and to the right of center, posters from Dennis Brown, Ken Eberts, Jack Juratovic, and Ken Dallison are all visible.

Assorted memorabilia is everywhere: awards, buttons, badges, lapel pins, judges' ties, and photographs.

A plaque on the front table includes the poster text, and it hides one image that appears only on the original painting—an image of Glenn Mounger's 1929 Duesenberg J Murphy Convertible Sedan, which won its class at Pebble Beach in 1993. Marsh knew in advance that Mounger was planning to buy the original artwork to celebrate his first year as Concours Chairman.

Ultimately, Marsh has created a poster that challenges the viewer to discover ever more detail, gaining an ever greater appreciation for the evolution and heritage of the Pebble Beach Concours d'Elegance.

The original artwork for this 2000 poster measures 30 by 40 inches.

50TH ANNIVERSARY
PEBBLE BEACH
CONCOURS D'ELEGANCE
AUGUST 20, 2000
THE LODGE AT PEBBLE BEACH

2000 Ron Kimball

■ THE 2000 PEBBLE BEACH CONCOURS D'ELEGANCE INCLUDED A SPECIAL TREAT—AN ADDITIONAL POSTER that celebrated the Talbot-Lago Teardrop Coupés that were among the year's many features.

To distinguish this poster from the work done by John Francis Marsh, Concours organizers commissioned the first photography-based Concours poster in over twenty-five years.

They commissioned Ron Kimball, of course—a man who is one of the most published calendar and poster photographers in the country. Moreover, Kimball specializes in photographs of two subjects: animals and automobiles.

Kimball started taking photographs as a hobby back in the early 1970s. As a lark, he submitted a few of his favorite shots to a local calendar company, and they not only bought those shots, they wanted more. His career was underway. Kimball's work is now sought by top advertising agencies and designers throughout the world.

In addition to popular calendars and posters, Kimball's work has graced the covers of hundreds of magazines, and it has been used on U.S. postage stamps, in books, and even in movies. Kimball recently shot the still photography of an owl for the Harry Potter films.

Kimball's early work focused on a mix of subjects. Then in 1986, he was asked to photograph the Ferrari Testa Rossa from the television show *Miami Vice*. The car's sleek curves won him over, and he sought more and more work relating to automobiles. Much of his work is done on location, but he also has a drive-in studio.

For his 2000 Concours poster, Kimball was told he needed to feature a teardrop or a boattail posed in front of The Lodge at Pebble Beach. He could do that without leaving his studio. He had previously photographed a 1939 Talbot-Lago T150 CSS Aerodynamic Coupé in his studio. And he had also photographed the Jaguar F prototype in front of The Lodge the previous year. Using a computer, he merged the preferred automotive subject with the preferred backdrop.

"You always need to think of all your tools," says Kimball. "And a computer is an invaluable tool today. When I started as a photographer we just couldn't do what we can do now."

He produced three rough layouts for Concours organizers to review, and they chose his favorite—a partial side view of the car that emphasized its curves. Once approved, he set to work.

First, he revised the background photograph, removing the car that was in the picture, turning on The Lodge lights, and softening some features. Then he put the Talbot-Lago in the picture, reversed the image, and flipped key details on the car once more, so they would be in their correct position. The most difficult work involved meshing the two layers—enabling the background to show through the car's windows, creating appropriate reflections and shadows, subtly adjusting contrasts and colors so the picture as a whole was balanced.

"It's not a photograph, it's a photo illustration, an art piece," says Kimball. "I could have made the illustration more like reality, but as an artist, I wanted to add my own interpretation. There were certain lines I wanted to accent, certain things I wanted to say about that car."

A digital high resolution file, accompanied by a matching proof, was supplied to Concours graphic artists, who placed the final image in a frame and added the text.

The final poster, which is unsigned, measures 24 by 32 inches.

PEBBLE BEACH

CONCOURS D'ELEGANCE

50TH ANNIVERSARY

2001 James Dietz

■ It was during the 2001 Pebble Beach Concours d'Elegance, when Bentley was featured, that the real "Blue Train" Speed Six Bentley was unmasked. For decades another Speed Six, a very stylish Gurney Nutting coupé, had been widely credited with racing—and beating—the famous Blue Train in a journey from Cannes to London in 1930. But meticulous research suggested that a simple saloon by H. J. Mulliner (registered as UU5999) was more likely the car in the race.

The artwork for the 2001 Concours poster, created by Seattle artist James Dietz, honors both the Bentley marque and the unmasked Blue Train Bentley. The painting, entitled *Wheels within Wheels,* features two great Bentleys framing a cozy picnic near The Lone Cypress at Midway Point on the Pebble Beach 17-Mile Drive. The Blue Train Bentley is to the left.

Dietz highlights the bright work of both Bentleys, and numerous details. Note the view of rock and sea through one wire wheel!

It is the picnic details, though, that soon capture the viewers' attention. These details convey both a sense of nostalgia and romance. Certain items stand out immediately: the picnic basket with silverware, the coffee urn, the thermos, the bud vase with flowers, the Moët et Chandon Champagne bottle, and the three hollow-stem glasses. The pink open shoes and matching sun hat create an air of mystery, as does a leather bag with the letters W. B. (possibly for creator Walter Owen Bentley or for early Bentley Chairman Woolf Barnato, who drove the Blue Train to victory). A meal of chicken, fresh fruit, tarts and tea awaits the picnickers.

Foreground details add dimension to the story. Books include *Bentley: The Silent Speed Six,* Agatha Christie's *The Mystery of the Blue Train*, and various Michelin guides. One special photograph features two women golfers—four-time British Women's Amateur Champion Joyce Wethered and Pebble Beach native Clara Callender—who played a match at Pebble Beach in 1936. Other photographs show a Bentley boys race scene, The Lodge with a Bentley, and a Bentley under the wing of a vintage aircraft. The pièces de résistance, however, are hints of the era—personal treasures such as the signed framed photograph of Annabella, first wife of Tyrone Power, and the silver cigarette case signed "To Nick, with all my love," as in the Thin Man series by Dashiell Hammett.

Born and raised in Richmond, California, Jim Dietz has very clear memories of his first true artistic effort—a painting of a World War I aircraft, created with watercolors on typing paper when he was in high school. The painting was inspired by Floyd Gibbon's book *The Red Knight of Germany* —and by the receipt of a complete London Water Color set with ninety different colors.

Dietz eventually attended the Art Center College of Design, now in Pasadena, graduating with honors. Thereafter, he earned his stripes, freelancing as an illustrator for advertising agencies and retail operations. Designs for a studio that produced black-and-white car advertisements led to commissions for book covers and work with some major movie companies. With this increasing recognition, Dietz's career was launched. His paintings are now in the collections of numerous individuals, corporations, and museums. In 1996, he joined the Automotive Fine Arts Society.

The original artwork for the 2001 poster, which is oil on canvas, measures 30 by 72 inches. Its sale to Bruce McCaw benefited Concours charities.

EBBLE BEACH
ONCOURS D'ELEGANCE
DIETZ
51ST ANNUAL ■ AUGUST 19, 2001

2002 Nicola Wood

■ TO CELEBRATE THE CENTENNIAL OF CADILLAC IN 2002, PEBBLE BEACH Concours organizers invited artist Nicola Wood to return to paint her third poster for the Concours.

As she did in 1993, Wood situates her favorite marque in a setting that details a romantic story. In this case, a 1933 Cadillac Convertible Coupé has been driven to a spot that combines elements of at least two distinct Pebble Beach locations. The Lone Cypress is seen to the far right and a hint of Point Lobos appears to the far left.

Again, we see the rear two-thirds of the car. The majority of its lines and accessories date to the mid-classic era; a skirted front fender line covers the bottom of the dual side-mounted spare tires, and the car includes the torpedo headlights that became popular with the streamlined designs of the mid- to late-1930s. But Wood also chooses to include the taillights with the blue centers that were used later, during the custom car era of the 1950s. These taillights were outlawed not long after they were introduced because they were too easily confused with lights used on law enforcement vehicles.

The multibar rear bumper is further highlighted by the folded luggage rack and the skirted front fender chrome accent stripes. And the forward location of the handle confirms that it is a rear-hinged suicide door on this Cadillac.

Patiently sitting on the running board is a well-dressed lady wearing a red dress, hat, purse, and shoes. She also wears a fur stole, dark glasses, and white gloves, and she carries a scarf. She may be waiting for her gentleman, and her thoughts may run to "a gentleman never keeps a lady waiting." Or perhaps she has simply driven out ahead to select the perfect location for a romantic interlude.

Wood's signature leopard print appears on a hatbox in this illustration. On top of the hatbox, six long-stemmed roses are tied with a pink ribbon. Several petals have come loose and have fallen to the ground, perhaps from the heat of the day.

Meanwhile, out of the billowy clouds, appears Cadillac's mascot, her wings spread out as she soars over this idyllic setting.

Wood's signature appears in the lower right corner of her illustration.

The original artwork for the 2002 poster, which is oil on canvas, measures 40 by 55 inches. It has been sold to David Kane.

PEBBLE BEACH
Concours d'Elegance
2002
AUGUST 18 • FIFTY-SECOND ANNUAL
NY 35
8N 44 Z9
Nicola Wood

2003 Ken Eberts

■ THE 2003 PEBBLE BEACH CONCOURS D'ELEGANCE POSTER, CREATED BY AUTOMOTIVE FINE ARTIST KEN EBERTS, commemorates the centennial of Ford Motor Company. Eberts was the natural choice to create this work; he not only had four previous Concours posters to his credit, he was also Ford's centennial artist.

The front of The Lodge at Pebble Beach serves as backdrop in his work, and two great Fords and a luxury Lincoln are depicted.

The poster features a 1932 Lincoln KB Dietrich Convertible Sedan. Details on this classic beauty include large oval headlights and twin trumpet horns, white sidewall tires and wire wheels, dual side-mounted spare tires with side rearview mirrors, and a split windshield. The deep blue body of the Lincoln is balanced by the light canvas top, matching trunk, and spare tire covers. The front door is rear-hinged for easy passenger access. The car's license plate number, PB O8 O3, abbreviates the place, month, and year of the 2003 Concours.

In the background, a 1947 Ford Woody Station Wagon has just conveyed two guests from the airport to the hotel. The black of the station wagon reflects the green grass, in contrast to the ash and Honduras mahogany on the car's side and rear.

The uniformed driver can be seen unloading the guests' luggage. A stylish couple strolls across the foreground in lockstep. The woman is attired in a bright yellow suit with white polka dot blouse and matching white hat, purse, gloves, and shoes. Her companion is wearing a two-button light brown summer-weight suit with cuffs and more casual hat.

Seen circling overhead, against a clear blue sky, is a silver 1930s era Ford Tri-Motor aircraft. Its fixed landing gear is evident as it buzzes just over the tops of the towering pine trees nearby. From the reflected light on the vehicles and the angle of the shadows, it appears to be mid-morning.

The artist's signature appears in the lower right corner of the illustration.

The original artwork for the 2003 poster, a combination of watercolor and gouache, measures 30 by 40 inches. The artwork has now been sold through the Concours to Ford Motor Company, helping to benefit Concours charities.

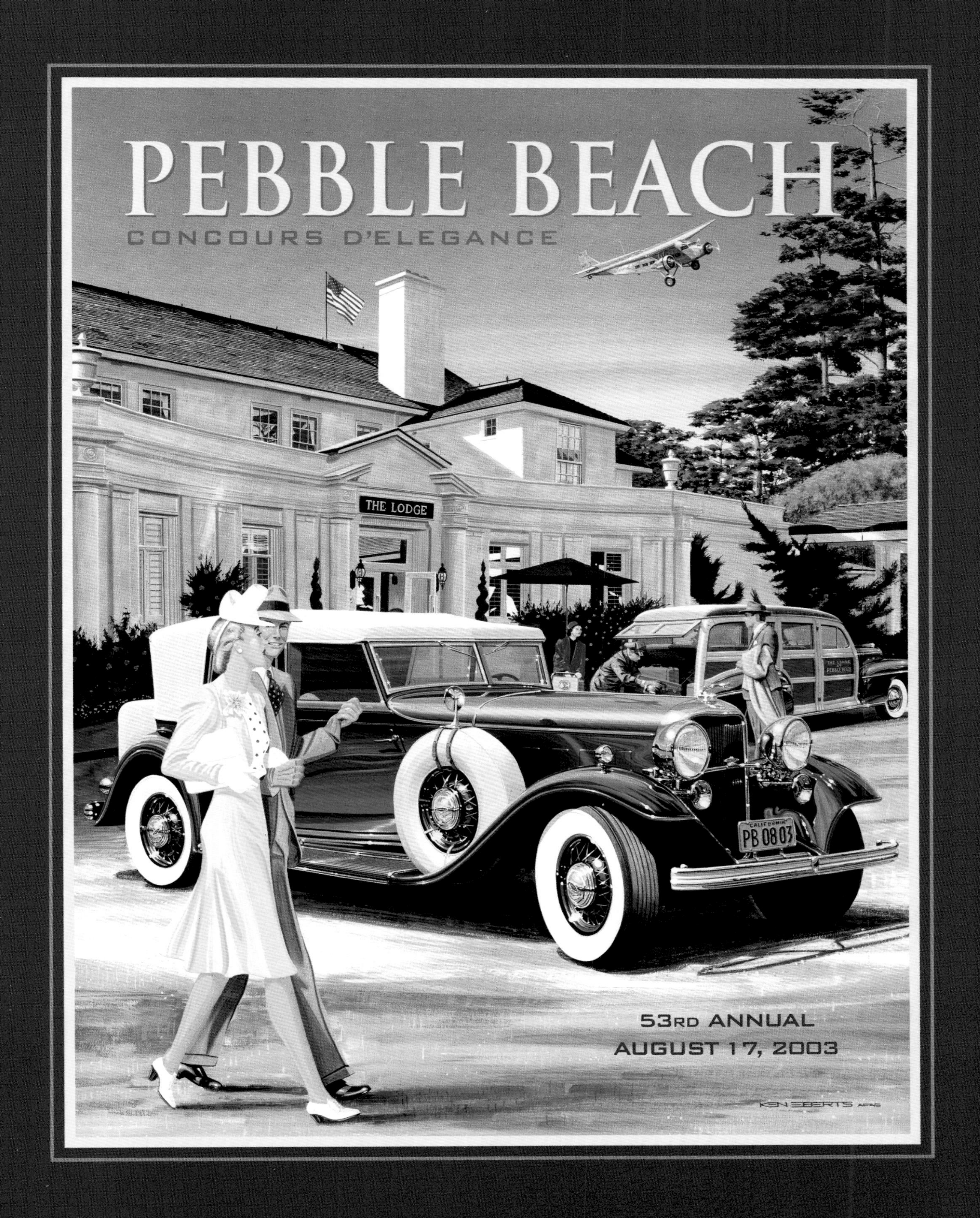
PEBBLE BEACH
CONCOURS D'ELEGANCE
THE LODGE
PB 08 03
53RD ANNUAL
AUGUST 17, 2003
KEN EBERTS

Posters from the Pebble Beach Tour d'Elegance 1999–2003

1999 Ken Eberts

■ Automobiles are not simply objects of beauty, they are created with a purpose—they are created for motion. With this in mind, in 1998, Pebble Beach Concours Co-Chairmen Lorin Tryon and Jules "J." Heumann decided to give Concours entries a chance to perform. They invited them to participate in a scenic 50-mile Tour of the area just a few days prior to the Concours. What better place to exercise a car than along the 17-Mile Drive at Pebble Beach? The Tour would also pass by Monterey's famed Cannery Row and quaint Carmel-by-the-Sea.

As added incentive, a new Concours trophy for Elegance in Motion would be awarded specifically to a Tour participant. And in the case of a tie in class competitions, the entry that had completed the Tour would receive the nod.

Seventy cars took to the road on that first Tour, and it was an immediate success. The Pebble Beach Tour d'Elegance is now an annual event.

Prior to the Tour's second running, in 1999, Concours organizers decided to publicize the event; they distributed posters, informing spectators of the Tour route. The posters would also serve as mementos for tour participants.

Concours organizers turned to automotive fine artist Ken Eberts to design the first Tour poster. Eberts had already done four Concours posters at that point, and each one had been exceptional.

Working in the medium of gouache, Eberts created an eye-catching piece with stylized background elements. The setting features The Lone Cypress, located at Midway Point on the 17-Mile Drive, amidst rock, sea, and sky. Climbing up an unpaved road, kicking up dust, there appears the 1934 Lagonda M45R Team Car of Craig and Bunny Davis, in British Racing Green.

The Lagonda is a roadster created in an era when racing and fast touring were the fad. This sporting model has cut down doors and modified cycle fenders without connecting running boards. Lack of bumper protection further attests to the car's competitive nature. The folded down windshield with small aero screens provides minimal protection to driver and passenger. Reflections of the passing scene are included on the left side of the right-hand-drive vehicle.

This artwork is positioned in the upper half of the poster with a black surround. Upper graphics are in sky blue, and lower graphics in gold. Regrettably those graphics cover the artist's signature. A map of the tour route is included at the far bottom of the poster, along with a listing of Tour sponsors.

The original artwork for the 1999 Tour poster is 18 by 24 inches. The poster itself is 10 by 26 inches.

PEBBLE BEACH

TOUR D'ELEGANCE

August 26,1999

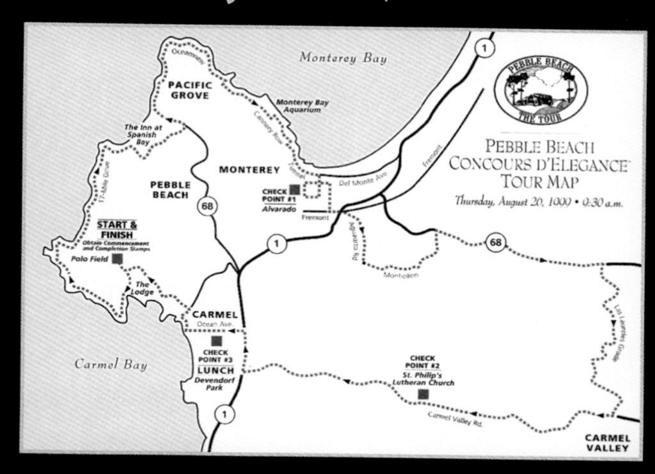

2000 Barry Rowe

■ HAVING SUCCESSFULLY COMPLETED TWO CONSECUTIVE PEBBLE BEACH CONCOURS D'ELEGANCE POSTERS, artist Barry Rowe was asked to create the poster for the 2000 Pebble Beach Tour d'Elegance.

Knowing that Maserati would be among the featured marques at that year's Concours, Rowe chose to depict a rare 1954 Maserati 2000 A6GCS Pinin Farina Coupé. The Maserati, driven by owners David and Ginny Sydorick, is seen climbing steadily uphill from the coast.

Details on the Maserati are well executed, and proportions are accurate. The Maserati has a grille opening reminiscent of racing cars from the same period, and the marque's symbolic Trident is mounted there. After the introduction of the Cisitalia 202 by Pinin Farina in 1947 at the Paris Show, major efforts were made to design a hood line that was lower than the fender tops. This was eventually accomplished with the aid of a centered and raised hood scoop to improve air intake.

An overhanging pine tree juts out of the left side of the painting to frame the receding coastline, and hints of shrubbery and flowers abut the car's right front fender. The sky is blue overhead, but it lightens to yellow at the horizon so sea and sky are easily distinguished from each other.

Rowe makes use of all the primary colors in this painting, and he also adds greens, browns, and silver grays.

On the poster, this artwork is framed with a mild red that complements the color of the Maserati. Some of the text is in yellow to match the lower sky, and other text is black for strong contrast. The bottom of the poster includes a map of the Tour route and a list of Tour sponsors.

The original artwork for the poster, painted with acrylics, measures 7¼ by 10¾ inches. The poster itself measures 9 by 26½ inches.

PEBBLE BEACH™
Tour d'Elegance
August 17, 2000
Monterey Bay
PACIFIC GROVE
Monterey Bay Aquarium
Cannery Row
The Inn at Spanish Bay
17-Mile Drive
MONTEREY
PEBBLE BEACH
CHECK POINT #1
Pearl Street
Del Monte Ave
Fremont
START & FINISH
Obtain Commencement and Completion Stamps
Polo Field
The Lodge
CARMEL
Ocean Ave
CHECK POINT #3
LUNCH
Devendorf Park
Junipero Ave
Carmel Rancho Blvd
Rio Rd
Carmel Valley Rd
CHECK POINT #2
St. Philip's Lutheran Church
Los Laureles Grade
Carmel Bay
CARMEL VALLEY
PEBBLE BEACH
THE TOUR
PEBBLE BEACH CONCOURS D'ELEGANCE™ TOUR MAP
Thursday, August 17, 2000 • 9:30 a.m.
Chopard
MOTOR TREND
Audi

2001 Barry Rowe

■ THE 2001 TOUR D'ELEGANCE POSTER, THE SECOND TOUR POSTER DONE BY ARTIST BARRY ROWE, FEATURES A magnificent 1930 Mercedes-Benz SS Erdmann & Rossi Roadster. This very car, owned by Arturo and Deborah Keller, went on to take Best of Show at the 2001 Concours.

The deep black car, with front pontoon fenders, external flex exhaust headers, multi-louvered hood, split V windshield, cut down doors, and external rear recessed spare tire, is a dramatic example of the German design of the period. To set this great vehicle in motion, Rowe has added a cloud of dust, reflections on the car, and speed lines off the wire wheel knockoffs.

In Rowe's painting, the Kellers, in white driving suits, cloth helmets, and goggles, are winding their way along the 17-Mile Drive at Pebble Beach. In the immediate background is The Lone Cypress on Midway Point. The headlands and Point Lobos State Reserve serve as distant backdrop.

Rowe has taken the elements of sea and sky and transformed them into a beautiful sunset with backlit clouds and myriad reflections. Note the interplay of shades of blue, green, and yellow.

Rowe's use of short strokes and multicolored layering is effective in the foreground on the rocks and on roadway surfaces. This more abstract application stands in contrast to the greater detail on the vehicle.

On the poster, Rowe's artwork is framed with the luminescent blue of the ocean. A cream yellow is used for primary text and black for the date. The bottom of the poster includes a map of the Tour route and a list of sponsors.

The original artwork for the poster, painted with acrylics, measures 7 by 10¾ inches. The poster itself measures 9 by 26½ inches.

PEBBLE BEACH
Tour d'Elegance
August 16, 2001
Monterey Bay
PACIFIC GROVE
Monterey Bay Aquarium
The Inn at Spanish Bay
MONTEREY
PEBBLE BEACH
CHECK POINT #1
Pearl Street
START & FINISH
Obtain Commencement and Completion Stamps
Polo Field
The Lodge
CARMEL
CHECK POINT #3
LUNCH
Devendorf Park
Carmel Bay
CHECK POINT #2
St. Philip's Lutheran Church
CARMEL VALLEY
PEBBLE BEACH TOUR D'ELEGANCE MAP
Thursday, August 16, 2001 • 9:30 a.m.
Chopard
MOTOR TREND
Audi
IN ASSOCIATION WITH FIVA

2002 Barry Rowe

■ Artist Barry Rowe's interest in all things related to Jaguar has deep roots extending back to the days when his father worked for that company.

For the 2002 Tour poster, celebrating Jaguar's fifty years of racing, Rowe chose to depict the Jaguar D-type that won the 24 Hours of Le Mans in 1956, driven for Ecurie Ecosse by Ron Flockart and Ninian Sanderson.

Rowe's attention to detail is evident; the color of the car is the appropriate shade of blue; it has a white stripe across its nose; its racing number, 4, appears in a white circle; its license number, MWS301, is correct; and the Ecurie Ecosse Club decal is on the car's flank, just forward of the driver's door. The driver also wears the correct Herbert Johnson–style, cork-lined helmet with racing goggles.

Rowe has placed this historically important car on 17-Mile Drive at Midway Point, with the famous Lone Cypress growing out of the rocky coastline. Another cypress tree frames the scene from the upper right.

Rowe uses various shades of blue to give life to the seascape, and he uses a brown wash on the headlands and Point Lobos State Reserve. Rowe has painted the Jaguar to show the best features of this high speed and functional race car. The car is placed at an angle with its front wheel turned slightly to the right to reveal more tire tread and wheel detail. A sense of motion is established by the dust and the spinning of the knockoff hub locks.

The poster frame for this artwork is bronze, with several black bands. The lettering is a light cream with a drop shadow. The bottom of the poster includes a list of Tour sponsors and a map of the Tour route, which has been expanded to include a lap at the Laguna Seca Racetrack.

The original artwork for the poster, painted with acrylics, measures 8 by 11½ inches. The poster itself measures 9 by 26½ inches.

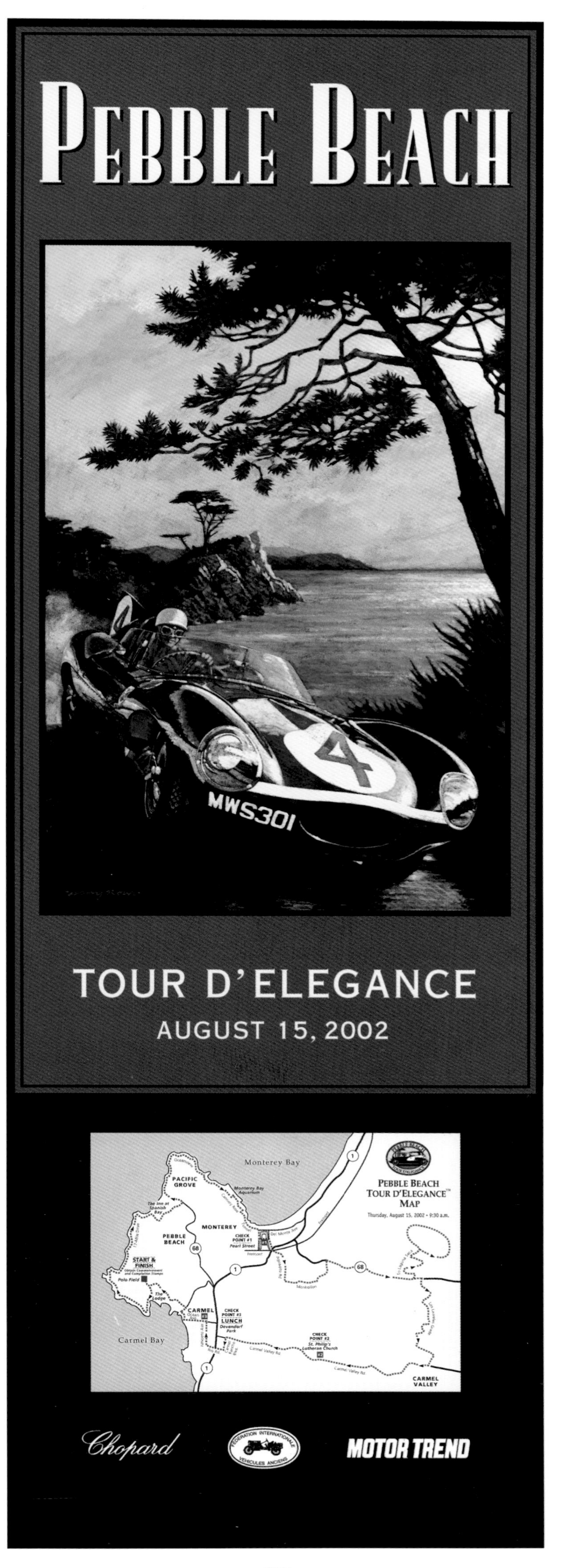
PEBBLE BEACH
TOUR D'ELEGANCE
AUGUST 15, 2002
MWS301
Monterey Bay
PACIFIC GROVE
Monterey Bay Aquarium
The Inn at Spanish Bay
MONTEREY
PEBBLE BEACH
CHECK POINT #1
Pearl Street
Del Monte Ave
START & FINISH
Obtain Commencement and Completion Stamps
Polo Field
The Lodge
CARMEL
Ocean Ave.
CHECK POINT #3
LUNCH
Devendorf Park
Carmel Bay
CHECK POINT #2
St. Philip's Lutheran Church
Carmel Valley Rd.
CARMEL VALLEY
PEBBLE BEACH TOUR D'ELEGANCE™ MAP
Thursday, August 15, 2002 • 9:30 a.m.
Chopard
FEDERATION INTERNATIONALE VEHICULES ANCIENS
MOTOR TREND

2003 Barry Rowe

■ THE 2003 TOUR D'ELEGANCE POSTER, ILLUSTRATED ONCE AGAIN BY BARRY ROWE, FEATURES TWO RARE Bugattis climbing a narrow dirt road away from a tranquil sea.

The lead car is a Type 54 sports model, complete with Bugatti's signature horseshoe radiator, large headlights, a multi-louvered hood, and beautifully formed peaked fenders. During the mid to late 1930s, these cars often had subtle multitone paint schemes, much like this one with a green body and black fenders. Two sporty looking men are seen in the car; both men have white cloth dust helmets and goggles, though only the driver is making use of them.

Following close behind the Type 54, is a Type 57C Aravis with low flared headlights that are integral with the flat panniers that extend out to form a modified pontoon fender. Again, there are attractively peaked fender lines with razor edge tips. Shown with a dark tan top, the Type 57 has a blue body, silver-gray side panel accents, and black fenders.

Rowe has framed these two rolling sculptures with various aspects of Mother Nature. In the foreground are low bushes on both sides of the road and red flowers are evident at the right. Overhead and to the left is a pine tree with several limbs hanging down. The sun is about to disappear over the horizon, setting the scene aglow in yellows and golds. The combination of sea and sky provides a backlit effect on tree limbs and foliage, particularly on The Lone Cypress at Midway Point on 17-Mile Drive. A sense of motion is evident in the dust that is kicked up and the angle of the Type 57 Bugatti.

The original artwork for the poster, painted with acrylics, measures 7 by 10¾ inches. The poster itself measures 9 by 26½ inches.

Pebble Beach
TOUR D'ELEGANCE
AUGUST 14, 2003
Monterey Bay
PEBBLE BEACH
TOUR D'ELEGANCE™
MAP
Thursday, August 14, 2003 • 9:00 a.m.
Oceanview
PACIFIC GROVE
Monterey Bay Aquarium
Cannery Row
The Inn at Spanish Bay
MONTEREY
Tunnel
Del Monte Ave.
Fremont
17-Mile Drive
PEBBLE BEACH
CHECK POINT #1
Pearl Street
START & FINISH
Obtain Commencement and Completion Stamps
Polo Field
The Lodge
Aguajito Rd
Monhollon
To Laguna Seca
CARMEL
Ocean Ave.
CHECK POINT #3
LUNCH
Devendorf Park
Carmel Bay
Junipero Ave.
Rio Rd.
Carmel Rancho Blvd.
Carmel Valley Rd.
CHECK POINT #2
St. Philip's Lutheran Church
Los Laureles Grade
CARMEL VALLEY
Chopard
MOTOR TREND
FEDERATION INTERNATIONALE VEHICULES ANCIENS

AFAS Awards

■ Each year at the Automotive Fine Arts Society (AFAS) exhibition at the Pebble Beach Concours d'Elegance several awards are presented to specific artistic works. The Peter Helck Award goes to the artwork that is judged Best in Show by the artists themselves. Athena Awards of Excellence are determined and presented by an independent panel of judges. And the exhibition's sponsors—first Infiniti (from 1992 through 1994) and more recently Lincoln (from 1998 through 2002)—also give out awards.

Pebble Beach poster artists have taken home these awards on numerous occasions, as the following table shows.

AFAS Awards Won by Pebble Beach Poster Artists

	Peter Helck Award	**Infiniti/Lincoln Award**	**Athena Awards**
Dennis Brown	1994	1998	1988, 1989, 1990, 1991, 1993, 1995, 1997, 1998, 2002
Ken Dallison			1990, 1995, 2001
Jim Dietz	1999, 2000		1999, 2000
Ken Eberts	1990, 1992		1990, 1992, 1993 1996, 1999, 2000
David Lord			1991, 1993
John Francis Marsh			1997, 1998, 2001, 2002
William A. Motta	1996	1993, 1995, 1999	1988, 1989, 1990, 1991, 1994, 2002
Barry Rowe		2001	2000, 2001, 2002
Nicola Wood		1993	1992, 1995, 1997, 1998

Index of Artists

Dennis Brown
1995

Dick Cole
1975 / 1980

Ken Dallison
1996

Eldon Dedini
1966–73 / 1990

James Dietz
2001

Ken Eberts
1986–88 / 1994 / 2003 /
Tour Poster for 1999

Julian P. Graham
1951–54 / 1958–59 /
1961–64

Julian P. Graham
William C. Brooks
1955 / 1965 / 1974

Julian P. Graham Jr.
1956

Ed Greco
1976

Bill Hinds
1977

Jack Juratovic
1991

Index of Artists continued

Hank Ketcham
1979

Dong Sun Kim
1978

Ron Kimball
2000

David Lord
1989

Loralee Lyman
1985

John Francis Marsh
2000

William A. Motta
1992

Jim Miller
1981–82

Barry Rowe
1998–99
Tour posters for 2000–03

Picture
not
Available

John Courtney Sandefur
1950

Thom Thomas
1983–1984

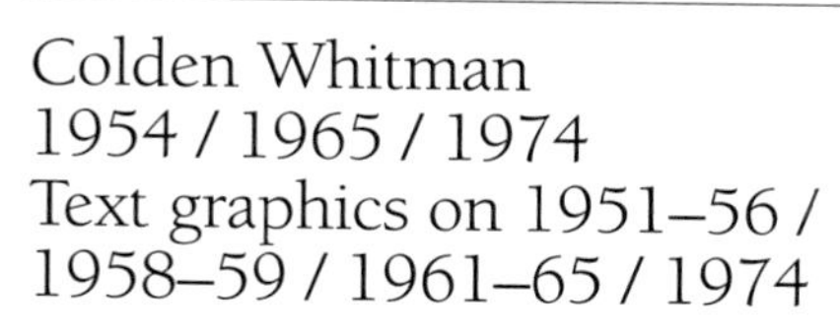

Colden Whitman
1954 / 1965 / 1974
Text graphics on 1951–56 /
1958–59 / 1961–65 / 1974

Nicola Wood
1993 / 1997 / 2002

Artist Unknown
1957

■ WHAT IS IT ABOUT THE AUTOMOBILE THAT SO CAPTURES OUR IMAGINATION, OUR PASSION, OUR INTELLECT? What other tool born out of utility has come to so often be an object of desire and dreams? We suggest the answer is that the car symbolizes the freedom to go where we want when we want. It is also a fashion statement. And, it is often a reflection of who we are, sometimes even an image of who we would like to be.

The Pebble Beach Concours d'Elegance presents each year a rarified yet embracing celebration of the automobile in its most stylish, most beautiful, most outrageous, most uncommon forms. Staged against the natural beauty of the Monterey coast, the Concours draws enthusiasts with as much personality as the cars on display. The mix is intoxicating, refined yet electric, bold but nuanced.

The artists who have created the original artwork used each year for the Pebble Beach Concours poster have portrayed all these qualities in ways that are different each year, yet consistent in capturing the many sensual pleasures of the automobile. Each work is a short story into which the viewer can add his or her own dialogue. It is exactly this aspect of personal fantasy that is, we think, at the center of why the car so intrigues us.

We thank Ford Motor Company for their support of both this book and the charities that the Concours supports, which include: The Pebble Beach Company Foundation, United Way of Monterey County, The Wheelchair Foundation, and the Boys & Girls Club of Monterey County. So, know that as you are enjoying yourself you are also helping others.

Sit back, turn the pages and get ready to drift down a number of roads. We know you'll have a great ride.

Glenn Mounger

Sandra Kasky

Co-Chairmen
Pebble Beach Concours d'Elegance

Blackhawk 

A great admirer of the artwork that has produced magnificent posters at the Pebble Beach Concours d'Elegance, Don Williams of the Blackhawk Collection is delighted to have supported this book and to have assisted in its preparation.

For over 50 years the Pebble Beach Concours d'Elegance has grown to a position of pre-eminence not only as a classic car event, but as an event where the automobile, as an art form, is held in the highest regard. The Concours posters featured in this book have become highly desirable. Blackhawk Collection is delighted to be able to offer a limited edition series of all these posters.

Blackhawk
COLLECTION

Donald E. Williams
1092 Eagles Nest Place
Danville, California 94506
Phone: (925) 736-3444
Fax: (925) 736-4375

Posters displayed in this book may be obtained at:

Blackhawk

1092 Eagles Nest Place, Danville, California 94506
Tel: 1 925 736 3444 • Fax: 1 925 736 4375
www.BlackhawkCollection.com

Page Size: 330mm x 240mm
Body text set in 11 / 14pt Berkeley Book
Titles set in 56pt (Year) and 36pt (Artists Name) Diotima Roman
Text paper is Sovereign Gloss 200gsm
End papers printed on Huntsman Silk Ivory 135gsm
Printed in four color litho on a Heidelberg Speedmaster 102 5 color press
Fishburn Flashdri process inks
Case bound in Wibalin Buckram 588
Dustjacket printed in four color litho on Sovereign Gloss 130gsm
Pre-press studio work and printing by Lavenham Press, Suffolk, England